LANGUAGE COACHING IN ACTION

Brain-friendly materials using Neurolanguage Coaching

© 2017 Rachel Marie Paling pdf version
© 2023 Rachel Marie Paling edited print version
www.neurohearteducation.com
www.efficientlanguagecoaching.com
info@efficientlanguagecoaching.com
For any information on courses and updates:
www.languagecoachingcertification.com
Copies of these works have been lodged to protect the copyright of the author, according to
copyright laws in force in the USA, Germany and the UK.

ELC Efficient Language Coaching®, ELC Language Coaching Certification ®and
Neurolanguage Coaching®
are registered trademarks owned by
Rachel M. Paling and Efficient Language Coaching Ltd

All rights reserved. No part of this publication may be reproduced or transmitted in any form or by any means, electronic or mechanical including photocopying, recording or any information storage or retrieval system, without prior permission in writing from the publishers.

The right of Rachel Paling to be identified as the author of this work has been asserted by her in accordance with the Copyright, Designs and Patents Act 1988

First published in the United Kingdom in 2023 by
The Choir Press

ISBN 978-1-78963-418-1

I never teach my pupils, I only attempt to provide the conditions in which they can learn.

Albert Einstein

To have another language is to possess a second soul.

Charlemagne

AIMING TO PROVOKE BRAIN CONNECTIONS

Note from Rachel

The objective behind these brain-based materials is to provoke and stimulate language connections for the learner of English, assisting the learner to build bridges, associate and group as much as possible.

As expert language educators, I am sure that you have the experience of all grammatical areas and this book is about bringing in different angles and different thought-provoking ideas that are brain-friendly and communicated through coaching conversations: all with the aim of assisting patterning and new neural connections and "making it stick" in long-term memory more and more. When we change the way we deliver through a coaching style of communication, then the magic starts to happen.

T. Doyle, neuroscientist, states "the one who does the work, is, in fact, the one who does the learning!" – so the IDEAL scenario is that you cocreate materials with the learner or the learner creates the materials with your powerful coaching questions to help ask the right questions though that creation process.

So, this is about you, the language coach or neurolanguage coach, using the visuals as the stimuli to then re-create them; change them; elaborate on them; get your coachee to create them in their own visual style or get your coachee to create their own flow charts, diagrams etc based on what they are seeing here. Through that creation process, the impacting coaching conversations help create more "aha" moments and more impacting imprints of the rules and theory.

In particular, the materials aim to bring THE BIG PICTURE of grammar areas to learners. This will mean they will have more of an overview which will bring them certainty to each topic, with clear beginnings and endings of grammar areas and enable them to "join the dots" much more. This is especially the case for the visual overviews of all the tenses (both active and passive overviews), so that the learner can in fact see ALL of the tenses together and how they interact and interplay with each other, instead of disjointed time lines that do not connect in the learner's mind. So, the real desire here is to help our learners see the big picture and help them to break it down.

My final words in this prologue, would be to encourage you to constantly be asking the following question: "How can I really help my coachee to constantly make new neural connections in this grammar topic?"

Wishing you all the best in your (Neuro)language Coaching sessions.
Rachel

How to use the PACT PQC©[1] coaching model to navigate grammar through Coaching Conversations

Back in 2012 when I was creating the method and approach called Neurolanguage Coaching, I created a coaching model that would allow continuous flow and interaction with learners, allowing a fluid, effective conversation that would really impact their capacity to understand, learn and imprint grammar. What I had not realised at that point, was that this model can in fact be applied to non-grammar topics and, in addition, also to the « delivery » of materials. For this reason, this book not only introduces some ideas for « brain-based materials », but also gives comments and example conversations relating to how we can « sit in the space » with our learner and then flow into the coaching conversation using the model and be present with the co-creation of the materials with the learner. Coaching *per se* is about being spontaneous, about following the coachee and getting the coachee to carve his or her own pathway or bring out his/her own knowledge. How is it possible to combine this with the idea of the teacher teaching and passing knowledge and information to the learner?

Well, yes it really is possible! By changing the way we communicate with learners and by introducing the new information through a non-directive coaching style, we can in fact maintain a coaching approach throughout. The neuroscientific research also clearly evidences that non-directive coaching is key for the stimulation and production of creative « insights » and induces higher levels of creative ideas. (Bartolomé Gorka, Vila Sergi, Torrelles-Nadal Cristina, Blanco Eduardo, Right Cortical Activation During Generation of Creative Insights: An Electroencephalographic Study of Coaching, Frontiers in Education VOLUME 7, 2022).

In this way, we bridge the dichotomy that arises when comparing teaching and coaching and the two become one with a flowing, insight-provoking, dancing conversation.

As an introduction to the PACT PQC model I would like to

- explain what I mean by professional coaching and how this has evolved over the last fifty years;

- introduce the integration of professional coaching and neuroscientific principles into the language learning process;

- give more information about coaching models in general and their efficiency;

- introduce PACT PQC as the new coaching model for language and educational coaching conversations I created in 2012.

---

[1] Copyright Rachel Marie Paling 2012

Professional coaching and how this has evolved over the last fifty years

The word « coaching » seems to be in vogue. The word itself originates from the Hungarian language and signifies a « form of transport », and very much portrays the feeling of getting someone from point A to point B. In essence, this is exactly the philosophy behind coaching: assisting someone to move from their starting point and arrive at their desired destination. In the 15th /16th centuries there are traces that the word was used for a private tutor.

Of course, the most prominent use of this word has been in the sports' world and we all conjure up the image of the football or basketball coach. In fact, the figure of the sports coach is that leader of the team who steers, trains, coordinates, cheers, challenges and pushes the team members beyond limits. In this respect, we could definitely say that the sports coach is quite directive, demanding and at times could use « tough love » tactics.

In the 1970s, the development of life coaching relating to personal goals and business/professional coaching started to develop. However, I would suggest that the essence and philosophy of this type of coaching was and is very different to the figure of the sports coach! This new emergent figure of the life/business coach is the person acting as a « sound board », a facilitator, a *provocateur* who is stimulating the coachee to reveal and discover own insights, setting own goals and actions and really being encouraged to be in the driver's seat of his or her life. Obviously, there are different styles and approaches to coaching and some coaches may also have a field of expertise where they may share that expertise, but normally not in a directive or forceful way. The coach may introduce coaching techniques, models and specialised coaching tools to enhance the coachee's « discovery of self » process.

This wave of life and business coaching began in the US and then came over to the UK in the 90s and now we are witnessing the wave of « coaching » right across the world. As such, the coaching profession has developed as an unregulated business, and that is still the case in 2023. However, over the years, certain institutions or standardising bodies were created or founded, such as the International Coach Federation (ICF) in 1994; a non-profit organisation created to set out the guidelines, standards, training competences and ethics for the coaching profession. The ICF have credentials for professional coaches and also accreditations for programmes that prove to follow ICF competences and standards.

We can safely say that nowadays the phenomenon of coaching has penetrated all walks of life. Not only life and business, but we also hear of executive, team, health, career and many, many more and now we have the phenomenon of language coaching.

At this point, I would like to bring in different discussions relating to coaching. Firstly, we have to recognise that anyone in the world can call themselves a « coach », from the sports world to the professional and educational arenas, it really is possible. (As an aside, may I also point out that in fact anyone could also call themselves a « teacher ».)

We also need to add that coaching has also been present in education for the past thirty years. Educational coaching and instructional coaching are both different approaches to integrating coaching into schools and teaching. However, these mostly focus on coaching teachers to troubleshoot processes, administration and also deliver more effective teaching techniques and processes. Many universities have also had modules on coaching in their Masters or PhD degree programmes, so coaching has slowly been seeping into the academic and educational field for quite a while now. In some countries, there are further education institutions that offer coaching programmes that go deeply into psychology, often with in-depth courses that take three to five years to accomplish.

Concluding on all of this, could we then say coaches could be classified into the following categories (and at this point I would just like to add that there is no insinuation of better or worse, just a factual discernment of types of coaches):

> ➢ Anyone calling themselves a coach, with great experience in their field, but maybe no formal qualifications and acts in the light of the spirit of the sports coach; that is someone who is encouraging someone else to achieve something but with no formal coach training from an institution or body that standardises professional coaching.

> ➢ Someone who is an expert in their field with qualifications in that field (such as a qualified lawyer or chartered accountant) calling themselves a coach but with no formal or academic coaching training from an institution or body that standardises professional coaching.

> ➢ Someone who has undergone an academic module in coaching at university or a full university /further education degree or course which also covers areas such as psychology and/or educational psychology / but has not done any coaching training from an institution or body that standardises professional coaching.

> ➢ Someone who has received coaching training from an institution or body that standardises professional coaching such as the ICF and in this case, this could be an ICF credentialed coach or someone who has taken a programme that gives the ICF accreditation

The integration of professional coaching and neuroscientific principles into the language learning process

Following on from the above, we can definitely see the development of the phenomena language coaching in today's language market. In fact, Neurolanguage Coaching® was born in the year 2012 with the pilot course in Düsseldorf with my team of 12 language teachers. In 2013, the first groups of teachers worldwide took the course in Paris, London and various courses online. Right from the beginning, this course was launched with the accreditation from the International Coach Federation and therefore one of the first ever language coaching courses to carry an accreditation from a recognised coaching body. However, Neurolanguage Coaching not only integrates professional coaching into its process, but also integrates and implements the neuroscientific research, neuropsychology and emotional intelligence, with the result that the former and the latter are woven into the language learning process. This means that this particular method and approach goes beyond just using coaching models and techniques and it has no grey area confusing language coaching with life coaching, as the full focus is to enhance, improve and learn a language.

If we look at the categorisation of language coaches, we could possibly identify the following types in the language learning market of today. Again, I would like to stress that there is no critique or judgement of any of these and it really is for the learner, that is, the purchaser hiring the service, who should decide which type of language coach he or she would like on their language learning journey.

- A language teacher who just uses the word coach following the market trend and following the philosophy of the sports coach, with an empowering style and possibly a directive approach.

- A language teacher with many years of experience and expertise as such, who takes on the word coach to demonstrate that experience. These are highly qualified language experts with an intuitively developed coaching style but normally no coaching training from an institution or body that standardises professional coaching.

- A language teacher who undertakes a life coaching qualification from an institution or body that standardises professional coaching and then applies this knowledge to the language learning process. Here, there may be a grey line between life coaching and language learning and it may be necessary to really clarify with clients whether this is a "life coaching" focus or a "language coaching" focus.

- A language teacher who takes a language coaching course, which offers knowledge of the techniques and models from life coaching using these to troubleshoot and enhance the learning process. These courses may carry certifications and CPDs (continuous professional development) for teachers but often are not accredited by an institution or body that standardises professional coaching.

- A language teacher who takes the Neurolanguage Coaching course, which integrates professional coaching conversations, the structure from professional coaching, the essence of being a soundboard and a non-directive coach style together with the integration and the implementation of neuroscientific research, neuropsychology and emotional intelligence, which are all woven into the language learning process as well as bringing metacognition to the learner. The course to become a Neurolanguage Coach is certified by Efficient Language Coaching and accredited by the International Coach Federation and also accredited by the UK Standards Office.

Coaching models in general and their efficiency

When life coaching began to develop in the 1970s, the first coaching model to be created, (and seemingly quite innocently without realising the impact this model would have on the world of coaching!), was the GROW model by the late Sir John Whitmore and Graham Alexander in 1979, although it was not actually made public until Whitmore published his book, *Coaching for Performance*, in 1992. The model is an acronym for the words goals, reality, obstacles or options and way forward. The way coaching models work is by laying out a pathway through a coaching conversation and thereby serve as a compass for the coach to follow that pathway and explore each particular part of the conversation. This enables the coach to manage the focus, the purpose and the outcome of that conversation and serves to keep the coach on track, who in turn can then steer, guide and lead the coachee on that track.

Since then, there have been a multitude of coaching models. To name a few, the CREATE and FEELING models by David Rock, OSKAR by Mark McKergow and Paul Z. Jackson, and CLEAR by Peter Hawkins (indeed, there are many, many more).

Definitely, we need to mention also the SMART goals model. This was developed by George Doran, Arthur Miller and James Cunningham in their 1981 article "There's a S.M.A.R.T. way to write management goals and objectives". This model focuses on how goals should have a certain formula for success: that is, the goals themselves should be specific, measurable, attainable, realistic and timely. One key point to remember in coaching is that we are looking to measure success and achievement. In this way, the more specific the goal is, the measurable it will be!

Life coaching models, such as the ones mentioned above, may be used by language coaches to set goals, troubleshoot the learning process or as conversational topics for certain clients to get them speaking, practising and using a language.

PACT PQC as the new coaching model for language and educational coaching conversations

In 2012, PACT PQC was the model I created to navigate through grammar conversations allowing the trainer/coach to maintain a coaching style and approach throughout. One of the challenges that we face as language teachers is that we mostly go into grammar teaching by following the way we were taught at school or university or by long explanations of grammar, then expecting the learner to « get it » immediately. Often during these conversations, the teacher is on automatic pilot expecting the learner to catch up and follow. The major difference that PACT PQC gives us (actually there are a few differences, which we will explore in a minute), is the teacher/coach can adapt and follow the learner's pace and not vice versa !

In 2020, my book called *Brain Friendly Grammar – Neurolanguage Coaching* was published (Express Publishing). This book explained the model and how to use it with grammar areas. The two- step process involves firstly breaking down the grammar area into a step by step, part by part logical breakdown and after that, building it back up step by step, by using the model in a coaching conversation. Just like the life coaching models, this model allows us to have a track through the conversation, however, it is not a linear « start to end » model, rather it allows the coach to dance in and out the model using the different parts of it according to the learner and according to what the coachee knows or does not know! In addition, the model ensures that we stay in « coach mode » all the way through, and, in this way, we do not slip into a directive teaching approach, as it keeps us in a non-directive coaching style.

The original idea I had for PACT PQC was to lead, steer and guide us through the grammar conversations, so that we would not need to use the books and in fact the teacher/coach becomes the « resource ». Through time, I realised that we could also apply this breaking down and building up approach using PACT PQC also for non-grammar areas and then my breakthrough and insight made me realise we can also use it when working with materials/co-creating materials with learners. So, all in all, the PACT PQC becomes the standard skeleton coaching conversation for all that we do as « Neurolanguage Coaches».

My *Brain-friendly Grammar Book* explains how to use PACT PQC with the grammar areas and now, this book demonstrates how we can use the model with brain-friendly materials.

Each part of the model has a reason and impact on the conversation. It stands for Placement, Assessment, Conversation, Teach, Powerful Questions, Clarification. We will now go deeper into each of these.

Placement

Placement is a synonym for « positioning » or « signposting ». Many times, as a teacher we launch into questions, taking our learner by surprise. This causes uncertainty and can also cause stress, fear and anxiety leading to our learner shutting down and even feeling stupid, when they do not know the answers. More often than not, we are not aware of how much stress we cause with our questions. Additionally, a lot of teacher training aims at developing the skill and art of eliciting. On the one hand, I do agree that we are trying to get our learner to make « connections » and have « insights », but on the other hand, extreme eliciting can really cause stress! What do I mean by that? Well, imagine that in the session with the learner today I want to introduce the present perfect and I introduce it by giving examples and asking questions using that tense. I do not inform the learner about it, I give no indication of the use or formation, I just go into examples and questions and then hope the learner will make his or her own observations.

With Placement, we consciously avoid making our learners feel uncomfortable and we constantly signpost or « place » our learner into the part of the grammar we are bringing the focus to. This is like a constant announcement of what is coming in the conversation, a little bit like giving a presentation and announcing the content of each slide beforehand and then summarising before moving on. We could say, then, that Placement is a constant announcing of what is coming next and then summarising what has just been touched on. This has a double effect: One, it creates certainty and safety for the learner all the way through and two, the constant announcing and summarising serves as a constant repetition, which also helps to embed the information and the learning.

Taking the example of the present perfect. I would announce that by explaining to the learner what we are going to do. I would have my breakdown ready and use that as my consistent signposting.

« Today we are going to look at a new tense, which is a bridge between the past and the present called the present perfect. We will start by looking at the formation of this tense and then we will look at the uses and after that the time indicators which hint that we should use this particular tense. … Ok, so starting with the formation, we will look at the way we form the affirmative sentence first. …Ok so we have just taken a look at how to create the affirmative, so now moving on to how we create a question using this tense…Great and now we will move into how to create a negative sentence… Super! We have now completed the formation and we have covered the affirmative, question and negative formation. Now we will move to the different uses of this particular tense and I would like to break the uses down into six slightly different ways that we can use this tense…»

When we are having conversations about materials or we are cocreating the materials with our learners, the Placement is still crucial, as you will be informing the learner at all times what you are doing and what you are doing next, plus you will be summarising constantly. Placement is the backbone of all of our conversations and may I suggest the most important part throughout. If we do not signpost the way through, there is a great danger that you will lose the learner along the way.

Assessment

After the Placement, we have the Assessment. This is also an unusual step for a teacher, because normally as a teacher we launch into our explanation of the grammar area right at the start. We are going to stop doing that from now on and the first thing after signposting will be to ask our learner, « what do you know about this? » Mostly as teachers, we are used to giving our own explanation of the grammar area, but this can be dangerous. If our learner already knows it, you run into the danger of him or her switching off from boredom and repetition! So, it is crucial for us to assess what they already know about it. When they offer the answer, you will hear if they truly do know it or if they know something but not all, or even if they have no idea. The most important part is that you then understand what your learner's starting point really is! Why is that important? Well, from the learning and the brain perspective, it gives you the understanding where to help them scaffold from or where to help them fill in the gaps or clarify or even to know that they are starting from scratch and they have no previous connection/association to cling on to. This should not be confused with eliciting. The main question here will be « what do you know about this? » or « how do we do this/use this? »

May I suggest that P and A, Placement and Assessment, are the most essential parts of this conversation. More often than not, we start with the Placement and may then immediately ask the Assessment question. P and A will be constants through the whole conversation.

Conversation

The C for Conversation could represent two things. Once we know the learner has some knowledge of that grammar area or maybe we introduced some new information to the learner, then we ask him or her to enter into a mini conversation with us to practise it and put it into use or we ask the learner for example sentences. In this way, we can then check if in fact the learner is able to use and apply that grammar area with no problem and if not, then we may need to go to T to introduce new information or to clarify and put right wrong usage.

Teach or Transfer of knowledge

Whenever our learner does not know something, so when input from the teacher/coach is needed, then we have to move into « teaching ». Perhaps it could be better to call it « transferring knowledge » from the coach to the learner. The major difference here is that we adopt a non-directive coaching approach to introduce the new information. That means we check with the learner with permission questions before bringing in the new. This has a double effect. Firstly, by asking permission and moving into that non-directive mode, it keeps the learner calm and feeling non-threatened, so this will ensure that there are no emotional triggers that could affect the learning. Secondly, by asking permission questions, we are in fact opening the door to the learner's autonomy. It gives the learner a choice to move forward with the learning or even to say no and ask to do something else.

In addition, we bring in information step by step but try and get the learner to instantly try and use it with the same examples or trying to create the « grammar » or language with new examples. This will ensure that there is a flowing interaction between the teacher/coach and the learner, and once again this also means that the teacher/coach avoids going into long explanations about new grammar areas or new language.

Powerful Questions

Throughout this whole conversation, we pepper two types of powerful questions. The first type I call « powerful coaching questions » such as:

How could you build a bridge here?
How can I help at this point?
What could help you here?
What examples could you think of?
What does this remind you of?
How are you feeling about this?

The second type relates to the fact that we constantly try to stimulate and provoke connections between native and target language. We know from the research in 2016 that when learning a new language, our brain goes to the native grammar structure area first to try and scaffold and connect the native to the target. To assist this process, we ask questions to promote and stimulate insights and associations, such as:

How is that in your native language?
How is that similar to your language?
How is it different?
Where are the differences?

These questions are really important, because they help facilitate neural connections. We know the importance of scaffolding and we know the brain is trying to scaffold from existing previous knowledge (native or even other languages that the learner knows) so the brain is trying to leapfrog to shortcut the learning. If I may I would like to clarify here. I am not saying that we should constantly talk to our learner in the native language. What I am saying is we should constantly ask about the connections or misconnections to trigger associations and patterning.
For example, a Spanish native speaker learning the present perfect could be asked:

Does this exist in your language?
How do you form it? so I am hearing it is with the verb haber and then the past participle, so that is very similar to the formation in English!
When do you use it in Spanish?
Is that the same use as in English?

Clarification

This part of the model reflects the constant reflex of a coach to clarify and reformulate back to check understanding and to check that the coach is in fact on the same page as the learner. We do this to check that we have heard correctly or that we understand exactly what the coachee wants to say and the meaning the coachee wants to portray.
In normal coaching conversations we also reformulate to make sure we are both on the same page or to recalibrate and adjust. In addition, by reformulating in a learning process, we are also repeating back and this also serves as a consolidation of the learning.

So, am I hearing xxxxxx?
Can I just check with you, do you mean xxxxx?
So you said xxxxxxx, is that right?

PACT PQC in action

Now, we have looked at all the separate elements of the PACT PQC model. The main point to remember is that the model is NOT linear – this means the coach will use all the different parts of the model as and when needed. The main constants will be Placement and Assessment, but the rest could be at any time and in any order and the conversation becomes a «dance» and a flowing interactive conversation. The beauty of this conversation is that it will totally flow around the learner of that moment. No two conversations will ever be the same, because each learner will have a different starting point and different scaffolding from pervious knowledge and obviously each and every one of us is unique to how we create connections and how we associate and learn.

As mentioned earlier, the PACT PQC model is used to take the learner through grammar areas using flowing coaching conversations and ensuring that the teacher/coach stays in that coaching mode and approach. However, it can also be used for non-grammar conversations and, also, when the teacher/coach is using materials or co-creating materials with the coachee.

The next section of this book will introduce you to some ideas of how to create brain-friendly materials. These can provoke patterning or clustering of information or can help the brain to create pathways through logical step by step mind mapping.

After some of the materials, I have added an explanation about how to co-create this with the learner or I have in fact created an example conversation using the PACT PQC. I have created the conversation from the perspective of the coach and you can imagine the answer from the coachee. Just to add, if the coachee is a low level, I would dip into the native language when needed. At the side of each line, I have highlighted with the initial of the model, which part of the model I am using, for ease of reference and understanding.

Finally, I am linking you to one of my demo webinars, where I have introduced and talked about PACT PQC, and, also demonstrated how to put the conversation into practice.

I hope you enjoy it! And happy PACT PQC-ing!

www.languagecoachinginaction.com/demo

It is the supreme art of the teacher to awaken joy in creative expression and knowledge.

Albert Einstein

TABLE OF CONTENTS

01. OVERLAP OF NEUROSCIENCE, TEACHING AND COACHING 1
02. SPELLING RULES 2
03. SENTENCE STRUCTURE IN ENGLISH 5
04. QUICK GUIDE TO ARTICLES 6
05. UNCOUNTABLE NOUNS (Brainstorm categories with coachee) 9
06. COUNTABLE AND UNCOUNTABLE NOUNS/SOME AND ANY 10
07. PERSONAL PRONOUNS 13
08. SUBJECT, OBJECT & POSSESSIVE PRONOUNS & POSSESSIVE ADJECTIVES 14
09. ENDINGS FOR NOUNS, ADJECTIVES, ADVERBS & VERBS 15
10. ADJECTIVES, COMPARATIVE AND SUPERLATIVE ENDINGS 16
11. ADJECTIVES ENDING IN -ING AND -ED 19
12. TIME EXPRESSIONS WITH DIFFERENT TENSES 20
13. LINKING WORDS IN FAMILIES 21
14. QUESTION WORDS 24
15. POLITE QUESTIONS - ORDER OF POLITENESS 26
16. RELATIVE PRONOUNS 28
17. PREPOSITION FAMILIES 30
18. ACTIVE TENSE OVERVIEW 34
19. PASSIVE TENSE OVERVIEW 36
20. WHICH TENSE SHOULD I CHOOSE? 38

21. TRIGGER WORDS FOR TENSES 40

22. TENSE BUILDERS 41

23. PRESENT SIMPLE 42

24. STATE VERBS GROUPS (Verbs of "being" not "action verbs") 44

25. STATE VERBS (Verbs of "being" and not "action verbs") 46

26. PRESENT SIMPLE or PRESENT CONTINUOUS 47

27. PRESENT PERFECT 48

28. PAST SIMPLE OR PRESENT PERFECT 50

29. IRREGULAR VERB FAMILIES 51

30. FUTURE TENSES 55

31. CONDITIONALS AS MATHEMATICAL EQUATIONS 56

32. REPORTED SPEECH - TENSE JUMPS 57

33. VERB + Verb in To INFINITIVE   or   VERB + Verb ending in ING 59

34. ING or TO? 61

35. MODAL VERBS 63

36. OBLIGATIONS - MODAL VERBS OF OBLIGATION 64

37. PHRASAL VERB FAMILIES (examples of how to create groups) 65

38. PHRASAL VERB PREPOSITIONS 66

01. OVERLAP OF NEUROSCIENCE, TEACHING AND COACHING

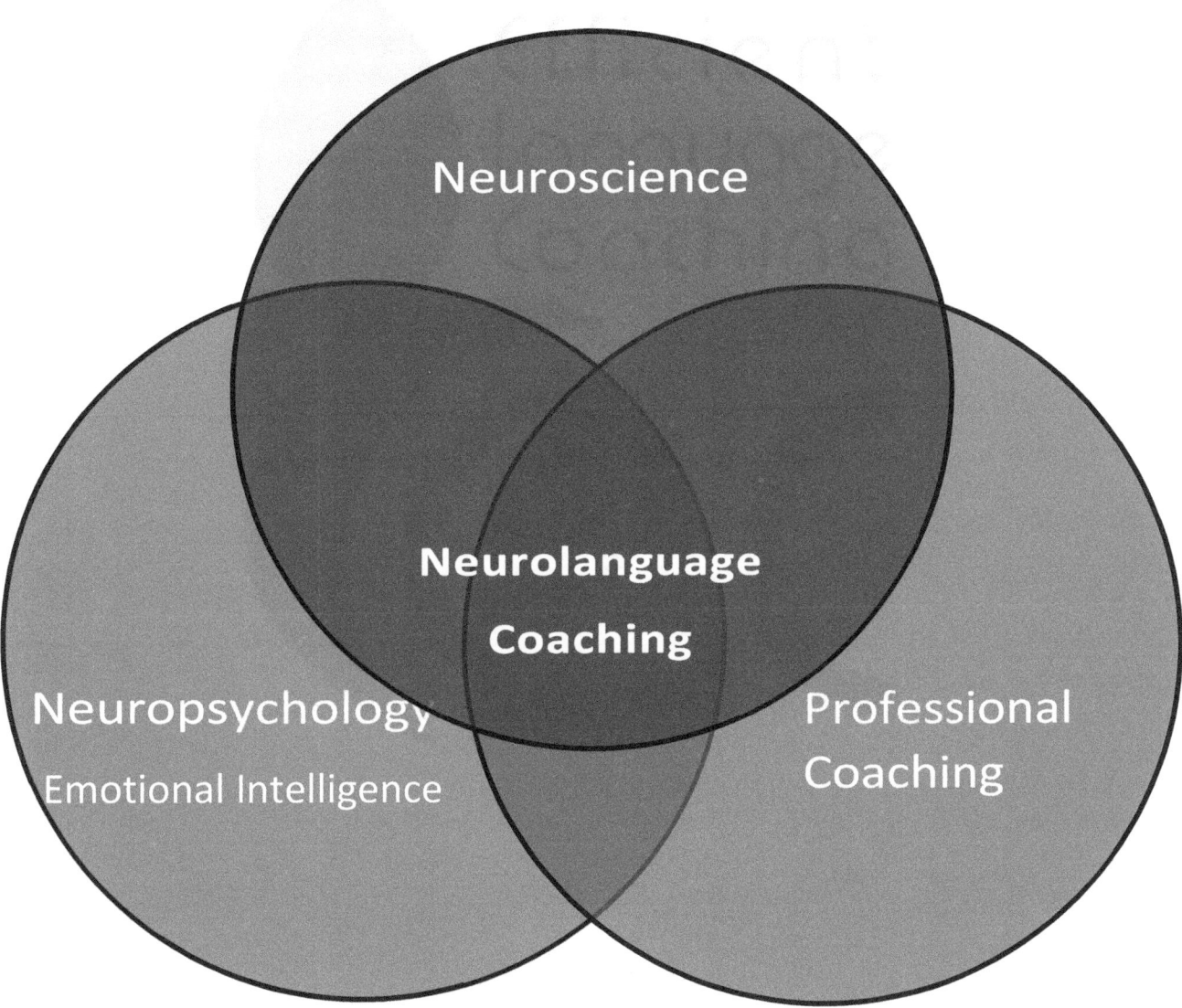

Neurolanguage Coaching encompasses professional coaching, neuroscientific principles, neuropsychology and emotional intelligence into the language learning process. This visual could be used to explain to the learner what the process is and what it really entails.

02. SPELLING RULES

PLURALS - VERB FORMS - ADJECTIVE ENDINGS

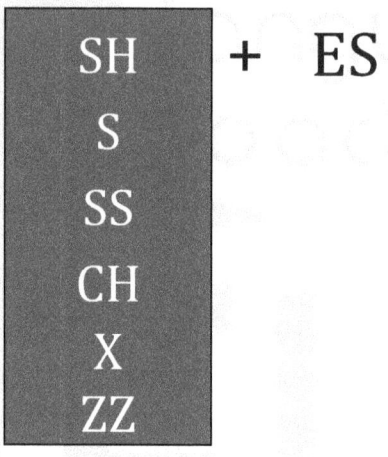

CONSONANT	+	0	>	ES
potato				
VOWEL	+	0	>	S
duo				
CONSONANT sky	+	Y	>	change to I + ES
VOWEL day	+	Y	>	S
E take	+	ING	=	ING
EE flee	+	ING	=	EEING

Adjectives one syllable = VOWEL + CONSONANT = BIG > comparative becomes double consonant = BIGGER

SAMPLE COACHING CONVERSATION
(These samples will focus on suggestions as to how the coach manages the coaching conversation and how the coach responds to the imagined answers of the coachee)

P – So, today we are working on your first goal to refresh the spelling rules for plurals, I mean when we add an S and when we add ES and may I add, these are also the same rules when we add the S or ES to the third person in the present simple tense.

PQ – How do you feel about working on these today?

P – Maybe we can start with the normal rule and then move to the exceptions?

A – May I ask you, how do we normally create the plural of a word?

CL – So, you are saying that we normally put an S at the end of a word, yes that is right.

C – Could I ask you for some examples?

PQ – How do you create the plural in your native language or other languages you know?

P – So we could summarise and say that the normal pattern is just to add an S to the end of a noun – boy, boys. May we move now to the exceptions?

PQ – How would you like us to create a visual demonstrating the exceptions?

P – OK, so we are creating a table with the exceptions. Now we are looking at when we add ES instead of just an S.

A – Which endings come to mind that need us to add an ES?

CL – You are saying the endings with S, SS, SH and CH – well done!

A – What other endings can you think of?

T – May I share a couple more that have not come up yet? In fact, the Z, ZZ and X endings would all need an ES after them. Can I give you an example? Fox foxes.

C – What other words do you know that end with an X?

C – How about we create a list of as many examples as we can think of with the endings S, SS, CH, X, ZZ?

P – So we have S, SS, CH, Z, SH, X, how would you feel if we create a table box as a summary of these at the top. OK, now moving into more exceptions. This time I would like to talk about "letter changes" and maybe we could create the table with the focus on the penultimate letter and whether this is a consonant or a vowel.

PQ – How does that sound?

P – Ok, taking the letter O first.

A – How do we create the plural when the word ends in an O?

CL – So you are saying that the word potato adds ES – yes that is right.

A – What about the word "duo? How do we create the plural there?

P – Just summarising that, we see that when there is a consonant before the O then we add ES and when there is a vowel before it, then we only add the S. We can add this to our table.

PQ – Out of curiosity, do you have similar scenarios in your native language?

P – Now moving onto the letter Y – we actually have a similar scenario!

A – What do you know about the spelling here?

CL – You mean to say that when the Y is preceded by a consonant then it changes into an I and then add ES, so sky, skies, but when there is a vowel before it, then it does not change and we just add an S – day, days.

C – What other examples could you give me with the letter Y at the end of the word?

P – We can add that now to the table so we can show the pattern clearly.

PQ – How are you feeling now about the S and the ES?

C – How would you feel if we now go into a conversation using as many words as we can in the plural … maybe we could create a story together …

03. SENTENCE STRUCTURE IN ENGLISH

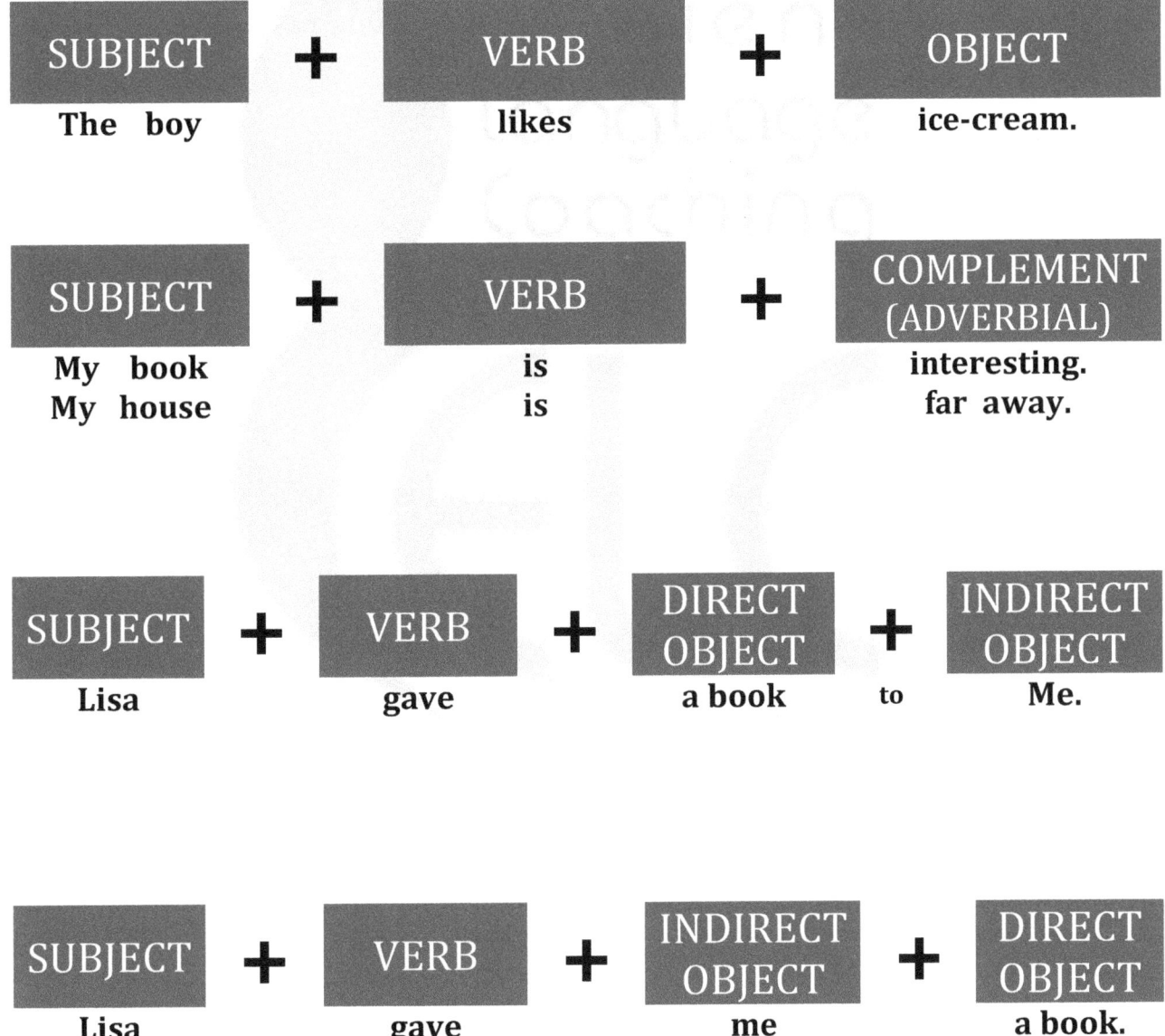

This visual can be reconstructed through a brainstorming conversation with the client, using the Pact PQC model. As the client becomes more advanced, more complex sentence structures may be introduced, starting from simple and then building up step by step to the complex ones. For example, the sentence structure of passive sentences, relative clauses or adverbial clauses.

04. QUICK GUIDE TO ARTICLES

First time to introduce a noun ?	YES ▶	A man
Only one item ?	YES ▶	A book
Is it expressing a general meaning ?	YES ▶	A method
Is there a specific item ?	YES ▶	The book
Is it a plural or uncountable with a general meaning ?	YES ▶	CARS (no article)

There was a man in the room and only a boy stood next to him. The man was smoking.
There is a book on the table.
It is a method which entails hard work.
Books can be found in a library.
The book on planes is in the lounge.

SAMPLE COACHING CONVERSATION

P – So, today we are working on your second mechanical goal to bring clarity to the articles and you wanted us to create a quick reference mind-map to help you remember when we use A and when we use THE.

PQ – How would you like me to do this? If I ask the questions, would you then create the mind-map/flow chart or would you like me to do it?

P – I would suggest to start with a really simple question to make it easy to remember when to use A.

A – Imagine you are telling a story and introducing the characters at the start, how would you do that?

CL – So, you are saying that to start a story, you would use A to introduce the character of the story.

C – Could I ask you for some examples? (Coachee answers, this story is about a cat.)

PQ – May I ask you, is that the same in your native language?

P – So, we could start the mind-map with that question "Is this the first time that this is introduced?" and then draw an arrow to YES and another one to "A". Now next thing we could focus on is quantity.

A – What would we use to ask if it is just one item?

PQ – And in this case, how would you say that in your language?

P – Great, so how bout we write that question and then the YES and the arrow to A. Moving on from that, we could now focus into the question of general or specific.

A – Imagine we are introducing something in general, which would you use then, A or THE?

CL – So what I am hearing there when you say A book is on the table, is more of a single item.

T – May I share with you an example of a general meaning? "I can mend a car in a garage."

C – What other examples could you give me? (Coachee replies "I can find books in a library.")

P – Great. So, moving now to look at the specific car, for example.

A – How would you then talk about specific things?

CL – So you are saying that "The book you bought is lying on the table."

PQ – So just curious, how would you introduce generic and specific in your language?

P – Just summarising that, we can ask the question "does it refer to a generic thing?" and then we could add yes and the arrow to A, and under that a NO refers to specific and then add THE.

PQ – And can I check in with you, how are you feeling about all of these so far?

P – Now moving onto our final quick reference question, we are going to move into plurals or uncountables and ask the question about general meanings.

A – What do we do when we have a plural or uncountable general concept?

CL – So you are saying that when we have something like a statement about doctors in general, we do not use anything. That is right.

C – What other examples could you give me like that?

PQ – Just checking, how is that in your native language?

CL – I am hearing it is really quite different then. In your language you must have an article but not in English.

P – So, we can add this as the final question on the quick reference mind map.

PQ – How are you feeling now about the basics relating to the use of A, THE or neither?

05. UNCOUNTABLE NOUNS (Brainstorm categories with coachee)

QUANTITIES OF SUBSTANCES	QUANTITIES OF LIQUIDS
Sand	Wine
Sugar	Water
Flow	

CONCEPT	GENERAL
Education	Sport
Information	Painting
Time	Noise
Experience	Life
Business	Night

Space

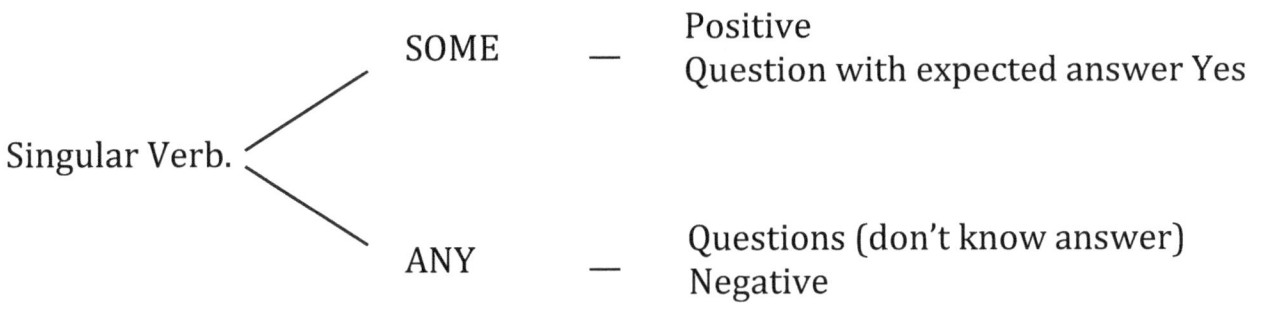

This visual could be created by brainstorming categories with the learner. The coach could signpost each category and then ask the coachee to contribute ideas and the coach could introduce new words through permission questions. It could be useful to keep adding to the list in further sessions, when words come out that are "uncountable".

06. COUNTABLE AND UNCOUNTABLE NOUNS/SOME AND ANY

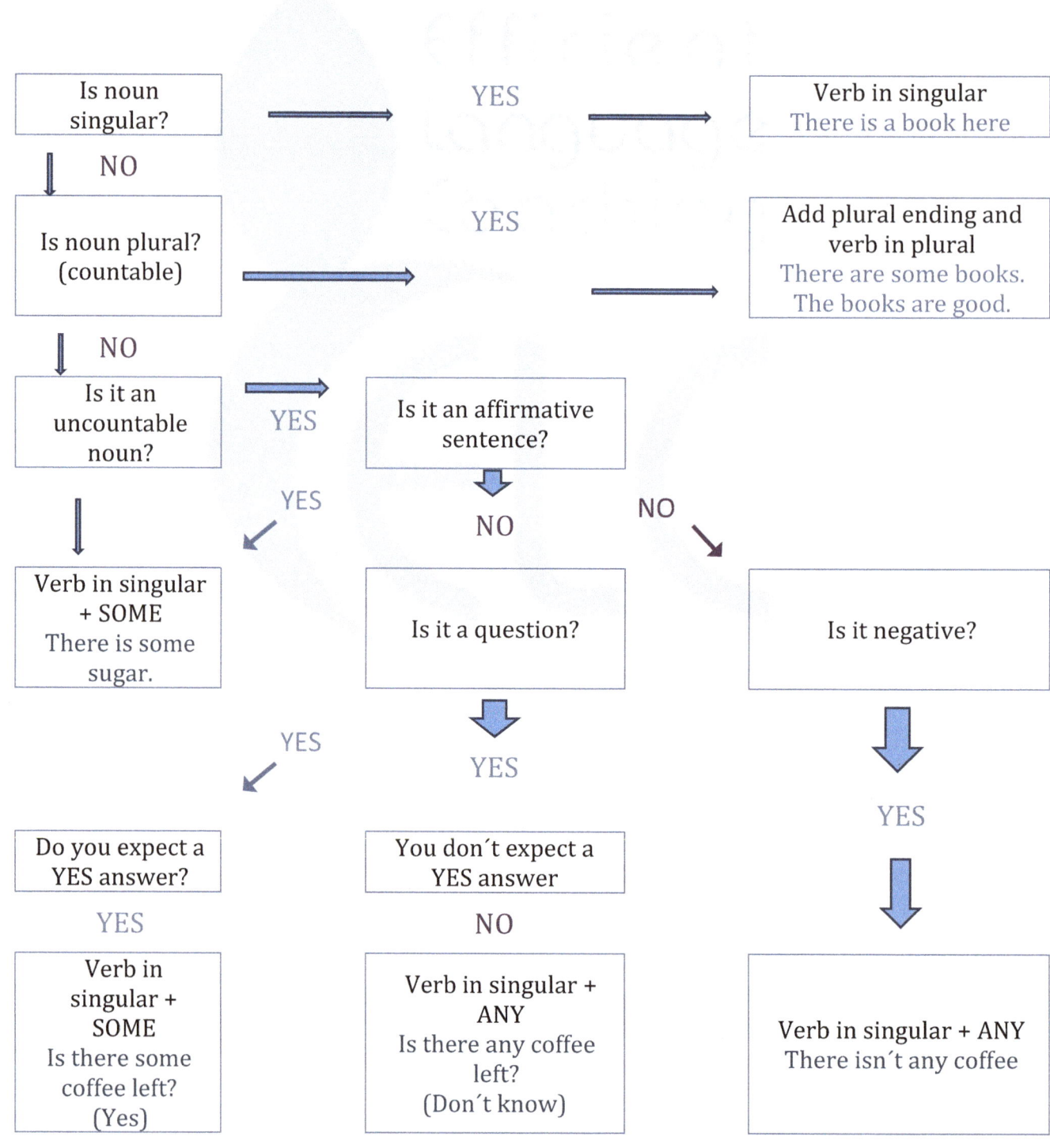

SAMPLE COACHING CONVERSATION

P - Today we are looking at the concept of countable and uncountable words in English. You chose this as one of your goals so that you could clarify which words would be classified as uncountable. You said you wanted to do this by creating a mind map.

PQ - How would you like this to do this?

P - OK so we will start with the questions and then create together the pathway through. Then I would like to suggest to start from the beginning looking at whether the word is in the singular or not.

A - What does a normal sentence look like in relation to the verb and the word, when the word is singular?

CL - OK yes you are right the verb also reflects the singular.

C - What example could you give me to reflect that? (The car is in front of the house.)

P - Super. Now moving into the plural focus.

A - What would happen to that example when we put it into the plural? (The cars are…)

PQ - Great. May I just check with you if that is the same in your native language?

P - Now we are looking at the word "cars" which is what we call countable, we will move the focus now to "uncountable".

A - What words come to mind when we say 'that we cannot count them'?

PQ - How about we brainstorm as many as we can and create a little list, especially those words which are useful for you to know?

P - Now we have the words, so let us look at a sentence with this type of word.

A - How do we form the sentence for example with the word "information"?

A - Well done, "the information is correct". Now, may I ask you, can that go into a plural form?

T - So, you are saying "The informations are correct" – may I say that actually in English we cannot say that, because we never add the S to the word information.

PQ - Can I check if that is possible in your native language?

C -. OK so I am hearing that this is a direct translation from your language and here we can see that it is not the same in English.

PQ - What could we do to help you remember this difference?

P - Now if we explore this a little more. We have said that some words like information are uncountable, now may I take this a step further and bring in the word "some".

A - When I say something like "There is some interesting information on that topic". what changes in the meaning?

CL - Yes, so you mean it gives a feeling of quantity. Well done!

P - On our mind map, maybe we could ask the question 'is the sentence and affirmative one?' And if the answer is yes, then we can use the above example with some. If it is not an affirmative sentence, then we could ask is it a question and if the answer is yes, then can I ask whether we still use the word "some"?

P - Well done. You are absolutely right, in fact we use the word "any" in a question.

T and A - May I share with you that sometimes we can use the words some in a question, can I check with you if you know when?

T – Ok, then can I share that if we think the answer to our question is going to be a "YES" we can use SOME.

C - What example could you give me of this? (Do you want some coffee?). Great example!

P and C -. And we can add that If I'm not sure about the answer, then I would use any. How about we reflect that onto the mind map, is it a question and then underneath, yes it is and I expect a yes answer, so I use some or yes it is and I expect no answer, then I use any.

P - Finally, we need to look at the negative sentence.

A - What do I use in that type of sentence?

P - Yes, that's right, we need to use "any". So, we can finish this mind map by adding this information about the negative sentence.

PQ - How do you feel about the pathway that we have created with this mind map?

PQ - How would you feel if we practice some examples now in a conversation?

07. PERSONAL PRONOUNS

Subject Pronoun	Object Pronoun	Possessive Pronoun (+ substantive)	Possessive Adjective
I	Me	My	Mine
You	You	Your	Yours
He	Him	His	His
She	Her	Her	Hers
It	It	Its	-
We	Us	Our	Ours
You	You	Your	Yours
They	Them	Their	Theirs

I see you with my eyes.		They're mine.
You saw me in your house.		It's yours.
He sees her in his house.		It's his.
She saw him in her house		It's hers

The creation of a table with all types of pronouns and possessive adjectives can greatly help the learner to clarify and compartmentalise the different pronouns. They could even be the comparison with the native pronouns to enable the brain to make connections and scaffold more easily. Tables may be more helpful for people who like logical and systematic approaches.

On the next page, the following visual would be helpful for those learners who prefer a more vivid visual connection with shapes representing the different types of pronouns and it could be useful to find out if the learner also responds well to colour schemes and for the learner to decide how to colour code the visual.

08. SUBJECT, OBJECT & POSSESSIVE PRONOUNS & POSSESSIVE ADJECTIVES

Subject	Object	Possessive Adjective	Possessive Pronoun
I	ME	MY (book e.g.)	It's MINE
YOU	YOU	YOUR	YOURS
HE	HIM	HIS	HIS
SHE	HER	HER	HERS
IT	IT	ITS	-
WE	US	OUR	OURS
THEY	THEM	THEIR	THEIRS

09. ENDINGS FOR NOUNS, ADJECTIVES, ADVERBS & VERBS

NOUNS	ADJECTIVES
- ment	- ful
- ion/tion/sion	- ous
- an/ian	- less
- ence/ance	- ic
- ist	- ive
- ness	- al
- ing	- y
- er/or/ee	- ly
- ty/ity	- able/ible - ant/ent
- al	

ADVERBS	VERBS
- ly	- en
- ize	

The creation of this visual is really helpful for learners to bring in patterns, which in turn stimulates the brain to "try endings out", like children do when they are learning their native language. It is also really useful here to use the PQ relating to native/target connection throughout the whole of this conversation with the learner. More often than not, there are patterns in the native language which are similar to the English endings. In particular, this is the case in Latin family languages and even in Slav languages, for example in Polish the ending Edukacja, Organizacja, Dominacja resembles the -tion ending in English, but then some words take a different ending, Przygotowanie (preparation), Oswobodzenie (liberation), Mnozenie (multiplication) all take the -enie ending. So, could there be a curiosity arousing PQ question to see if there is a pattern as to which words take which ending and if none, then could the coachee build up one list of all the English words ending in -tion with the Polish equivalents from the two Polish endings.

This type of conversation, opening the learner's mind to instantly understand the connections and similarities, will actually open the mind of the learner to a wealth of vocabulary instantly, without having to memorise anything. The learner will automatically associate the native with the target, of course, with the different pronunciation, but the word may indeed be the same word or the same ending!

10. ADJECTIVES, COMPARATIVE AND SUPERLATIVE ENDINGS

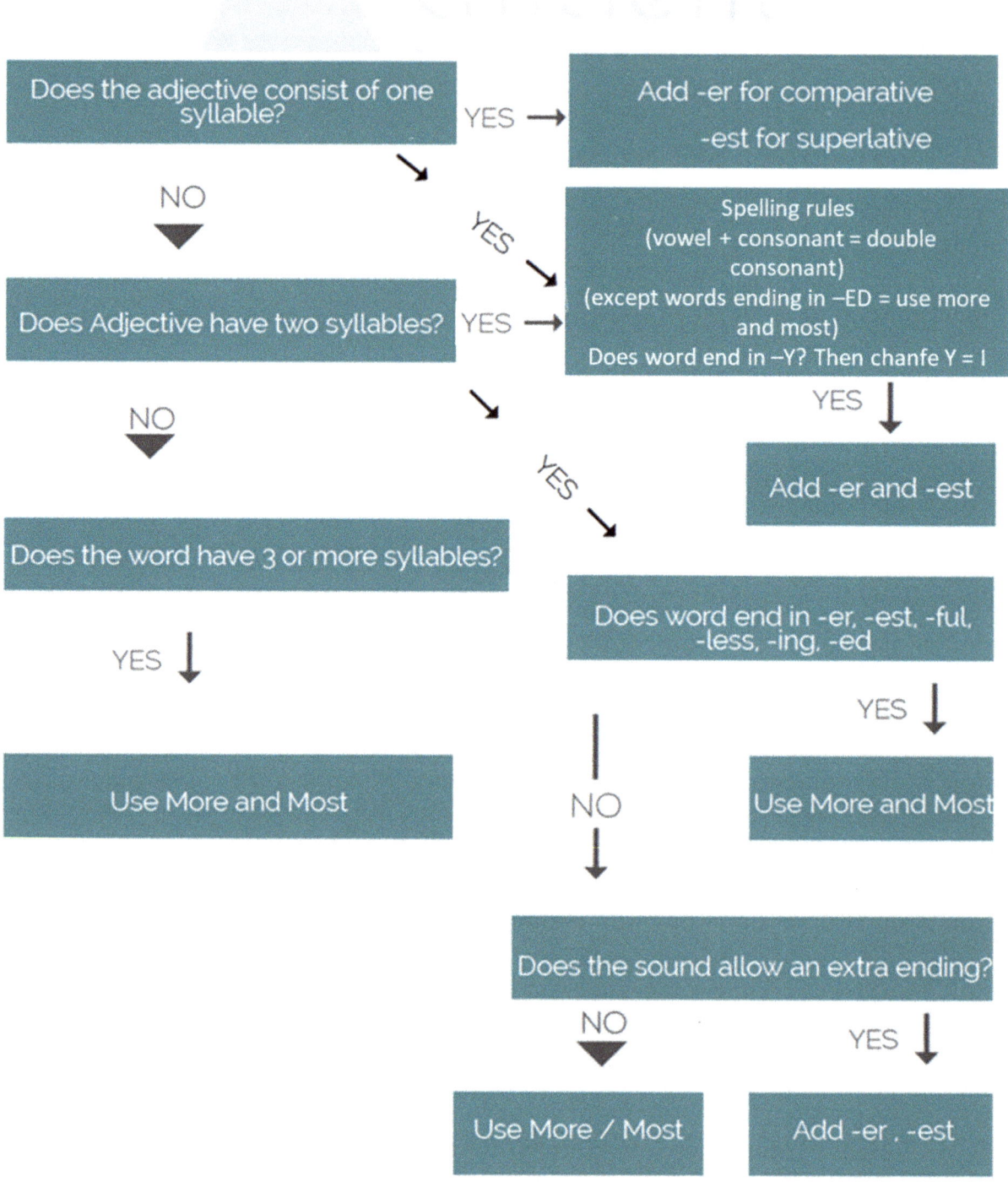

SAMPLE COACHING CONVERSATION

P - Today we had scheduled looking at your goal to master comparatives and superlatives in English. You had also mentioned that you would like to create a mind map to help you remember how we form these.

PQ - How would you like to do the mind map - would you like to draw it or shall I?

P - OK so may I start by saying we are creating this mind map around the normal adjectives and after doing this we will then look at some of the irregular ones. So, may I start with the question relating to the formation.

A - What do you know about the basic formation of the comparative endings?

CL - So, I am hearing that you are not sure about when the words take the endings and when they do not.

T - May I share with you, it really does depend on the sounds and syllables of the words. For example, if there is only one syllable, that is, one sound, like BIG, then we add the ending -ER.

C - What example could you give me using another word with one syllable. (FAT, GREAT, LONG.)

P - Super. So, we have the first question for the mind-map – does the adjective have only one syllable? If the answer to this is YES, then we can add the endings for the comparative and (T) may I share also for the superlative.

A - What do you know about the superlative ending?

CL - Great. So I am hearing that it is ER for comparative and EST for the superlative. Well done!

PQ - May I just check with you if that is the same in your native language?

CL - I see. What you are saying is that in your language you do not add an ending but you use the word "more" to form the comparative. Interesting!

P - Now, we have established that if there is one syllable, then we can add the ending, but can we now explore some spelling rules concerning this ending?

A - What could you tell me about unusual spellings when we add the ending?

CL - Right so you have noticed with the word BIG that we double up the consonant and then add the ending. Super!

A - What rule comes to mind then for this case?

T - Could I highlight then that when there is a one consonant at the end but before that, there is one vowel, then we double up the consonant. For example, BIG, Bigger, FAT Fatter. If that is not the case then the ER ending is added to the word with no doubling up. GREAT greater, WARM warmer.

P - So that is one rule we can bring out. Now moving to another rule.

A - What other rule could you think of relating to a change in spelling?

CL - So, you are saying that the Y is normally changed to an I, when we think about spelling rules. Well done!

PQ - How about we brainstorm as many as we can that are one syllable words that end in Y and create a little list, especially those words which are useful for you to know? (DRY, GREY, SLY, GAY.)

P - Now we have the words, how about we check the rule.

A - What do you notice when I say Grey, Greyer, but then Dry, Drier?

T - So, yes you are right and just to add, when the Y has a consonant before it then we change it to an I, if no consonant then we keep the Y in place and just add the ending after it.

P - If we put this into the mind map now, we can clearly see, if the word has one sound/syllable then we add the ending and reflect these spelling rules. Now moving to the NO, the next question then would be if the word has two sounds.

A - Now may I ask you, what happens then?

C - What examples could you give me of these? (Pretty, Orange, Silent, Quiet, Rapid.)

A - Now what would you say about adding the ending to all of those words.

CL - You are noticing various things here. Firstly, you said that the word PRETTY changes the Y to I, PRETTIER, well done! You also were not sure about the word SILENT and whether we add the ending or not.

T - May I agree with you and say that normally the words ending in Y, change into the I and add the ER. Then it really depends on the sound whether we add the ER or we use the word MORE. For example, SILENT, I totally agree with you that it would be better to day MORE SILENT and not SILENTER! That would really sound strange.

P - So, really we can summarise at this point that one syllable we add the endings, and two syllables, we normally add the endings, but there may be exceptions where it would be better to use MORE and Most.

PQ - Could we brainstorm these exceptions and see what comes up?

CL - OK so I am hearing that we could look at creating a list of endings like ENT, ER, FUL, EST...

T - May I add some more like LESS, ING and ED.

P - We can really conclude at this point that if the word does not have the above endings then we need to think if it sounds OK to add the endings or not. For example ORANGE would actually sound very strange to add the ending – so it would sound more natural to say more orange rather than oranger! So if we put this onto our mind map now, we have the different pathways that we can reflect here.

P - Now we still have the question, what happens when there are more than two sounds to a word.

A - What can you tell me about that?

CL - You are saying then that we add more and most and we cannot add the endings. Yes you are right!

P - So now we have the complete picture of when to add the endings and when not to add them. Now we need to just check in with some of the irregular words...

11. ADJECTIVES ENDING IN -ING AND -ED

This visual can be cocreated with the coachee by really taking the focus from extremely positive to extremely negative and exploring the different states that are being described. The provocative questions could centre upon the "noun" which then leads to the adjectives and the exploration of long-lived permanent characteristics or short lived states describing emotions or feelings that are transient.

(+)	-ing adjective	noun	-ed adjective	(+)
	Amazing / Amusing	wonder/fun	Amazed / Amused	
	Thrilling / Exciting	excitement	Thrilled / Excited	
	Fascinating / Interesting	interest	Fascinated / Interested	
	Relaxing	relax	Relaxed	
(−)	Exhausting / Tiring	tired	Exhausted / Tired	(−)
	Puzzling / Frustrating / Confusing	confusion	Puzzled / Frustrated / Confused	
	Frightening / Scaring / Terrifying	fear	Frightened / Scared / Terrified	
	Depressing / Disappointing	sad	Depressed / Disappointed	
	Boring / Annoying	tedium/anger	Bored / Annoyed	

12. TIME EXPRESSIONS WITH DIFFERENT TENSES

This visual is useful to highlight tense patterns after the adverbs of time. In many languages it is exactly the same pattern when there is a simple present in English: that is, a present tense directly after the time indicator and then the future. When there is a present perfect after the time indicator in English, in Latin family languages there is often a subjunctive or a future perfect (when you will have…). Here it could be really useful to connect in with the pattern on the native language in each example. "How is this in your language? How is it similar? Where are the differences?" and really helping the coachee to have a comparison native/target. The idea is to really help the coachee to connect with the logical sequence of the tenses here and cocreating this visual with help that visual consolidation.

WHEN
BEFORE

he arrives, I will prepare the dinner

AFTER
AS SOON AS

UNTIL
WHILE

I know the truth, I will not call
I wait for him, I will check my mails.

WHEN
BEFORE

you have finished, I will go out
you have finished, I will have gone out

AFTER
BY THE TIME

13. LINKING WORDS IN FAMILIES

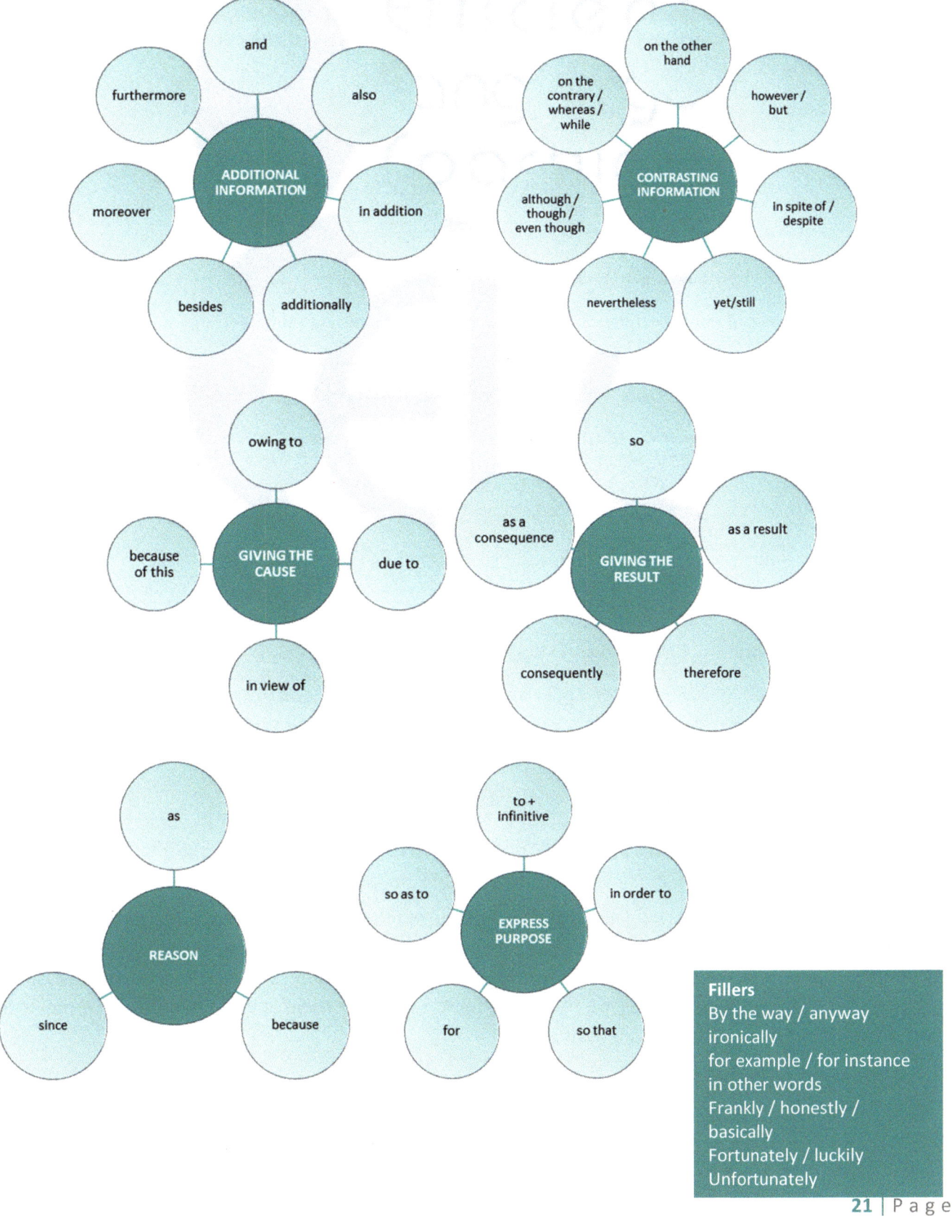

SAMPLE COACHING CONVERSATION WITH PACT PQC

P - So, today we are going to begin to brainstorm the goal you have set relating to linking words. How does that sound?

PQ - You had mentioned that you would like to create mind maps and categorise them into families, so how would you feel if I we establish the main focus of the category and then we brainstorm the family members around that focus?

PQ - How would you like to create the visual?

P - OK, so I am hearing that you could have a central point with the main focus and then we could have the related words around that central point. Super!

A - So what could be a first category and central point?

CL - Am I right that you are referring to contrasting information?

A - Great. Then, what words come to mind that really express a contrast?

PQ - Excellent, but, however, nevertheless, yes! So, may we illustrate this with the centre point called "contrasting information" and then start to create the wheel around with these words?

A - What other words can you think of?

A - Great – despite, yes! May I ask you if you can think of any similar ones to that? In spite of…. Yes!

PQ - So, can we put those together in one of the branches that comes out?

A - What other words could indicate a contrast?

PQ - What about in your native language, what would you say to show a contrasting opinion?

PQ - Well done, yes, we can say "on the other hand", and may I add some more ways that are similar – for example, "on the contrary", "whereas, while". How would you say those in your language?

C - What examples could you give me with each of those?

PQ - How about we reflect the structure of the sentences that you have just given to me as examples?

T - May I highlight that the structure of the sentences with whereas and while are very similar. They both need two contrasting pieces of information within the sentence. "Whereas I like tea, you like coffee. While I like tea, you like coffee". However (and here I am using one of the contrasting words from before), on the other hand or on the contrary, then have a comma and only introduce one contrasting argument.

C - How would you feel if we move into a mini conversation to practise all of these that we have talked about so far?

PQ - What topic could we focus on?

CL - OK, so am I hearing then we could focus in on food and drink ? Great!

C - (At this point, provoking the conversation with statements. I really love Indian food, however, I confess I cannot stand Sushi... So, whereas you hate Sushi, I actually love it! ...etc)

PQ - Well done, we have been talking for some ten minutes now. How did you feel with those linking words that contrast information?

PQ - Now, how about we add some more to this family of contrasting linking words?

A - What else comes to mind to express contrast?

PQ - Don't worry if nothing comes to mind. May I check with you by bringing the native word and see if you know this in English? In Spanish you would say "aunque". Yes exactly, that is the word in English! Although.

A - Now can I ask you if you know any very similar ways of saying that?

CL - Yes, well done! Even though and though.

C - How about giving me some example sentences with those? (Coach and coachee move into some examples.)

PQ - Now, we have covered quite a few words which contrast information. How about we put them all onto the visual and we try and group them so that it helps you to remember them.

T - (For more advanced learners.) Now just to conclude this part, may I bring in some words that as an advanced learner you could in fact use as "contrasters", although you probably know them with a different meaning. These words are Yet and Still. May I give you an example? "I love working, yet I try to really make sure I get brain breaks." Or "I love working, but still I try and have some brain breaks."

A - From these examples, when do you think we could use these instead of but?

T - Exactly, so these are more formal and definitely often bring in more element of surprise or emphasis to the contrast.

C - How about you give me some examples now?

PQ - Excellent. We are concluding now the words that introduce contrast. How about we move into another "family" now?

(At this point the conversation would then move to explore the next family of linking words – for example, linking words that focus on "adding information".)

14. QUESTION WORDS

Some years ago, I was in a conversation with a learner about the activities she enjoyed and found effective for learning when she was a child. She thought long and hard when I asked her that and then she remembered that as a child she used to love doodling (creating little pictures that helped her to remember). It could be interesting to introduce this topic, by asking the coachee how they would like to create the visual with all the questions, whether with the words, their use or whether with the pictures or even both words and pictures.

Powerful coaching questions such as:

How many question words can you think of?

How about we brainstorm as many question words as you can?

What can help you remember each of these?

What could bring in clarity to help the confusion between these words?

What are the words in your language?

What image comes to mind when you think of this word?

How could you draw something that would remind you of this word?

How could you distinguish this word from this other word?

How about you give me some examples posing questions with those two words?

I am hearing that in your language, the question word changes according to the case, how would we do that in English? (Special reference here "To whom…?" or "who…to?" "with whom?" etc.)

WHAT?	thing	📺
WHO?	person	👶
WHERE?	location	🗺️
WHEN?	time	🕒
WHY?	reason	?
What is the reason for	reason	?
WHICH?	choice	🚏
HOW?	way / manner	↻
WHOSE?	Possession	♜

15. POLITE QUESTIONS - ORDER OF POLITENESS

I	Most polite ↑	YOU
MIGHT I		WOULD YOU
MAY I		WOULD YOU MIND IF
		WOULD YOU MIND + ING
COULD I		COULD YOU
CAN I		CAN YOU
I	↓ Least polite	YOU

This visual really helps learners not only to brainstorm all the ways of asking polite questions, but also to clarify the degree of politeness involved, as for non-natives it can be really difficult to understand how polite something sounds or not!

Firstly, I recommend brainstorming the different ways to ask using I and then to brainstorm YOU (the difference would you vs could you is debatable in terms of politeness). With more advanced learners there could be a conversation about intonation when using some polite forms, which could lead to hints of sarcasm. There could also be another level of permission questions, when asking someone to do something. For example, "May I ask you to open the window?".

16. RELATIVE PRONOUNS

The creation of a visual for the relative pronouns is really to help learners understand that "that" can be used instead of who and which and nowadays, in everyday language, may even be used much more than who and which. It could be interesting to help learners that get confused with who and which to start off using "that" and then build in a visual to separate out who and which afterwards. You could also add to the mind map the question of TO WHOM, WITH WHOM and WHOSE (in languages with cases, the dative, instrumental and genitive) and then add the more usual modern uses, who…to? who…with?

Suggested coaching questions:

What could help you here to separate these out?

What visual or diagram could you create to help you?

I understand in your language there is only one word, and obviously in English we have three, so what could we do that will help you distinguish them?

How would you feel if we really create a lot of examples to consolidate each one?

May we explore some variations of WHO? May I share they sound a little old-fashioned, how could we change "to whom" into a more everyday way of saying this?

That was a great sentence using that, how about repeating the sentence but changing "that" to either who or which?

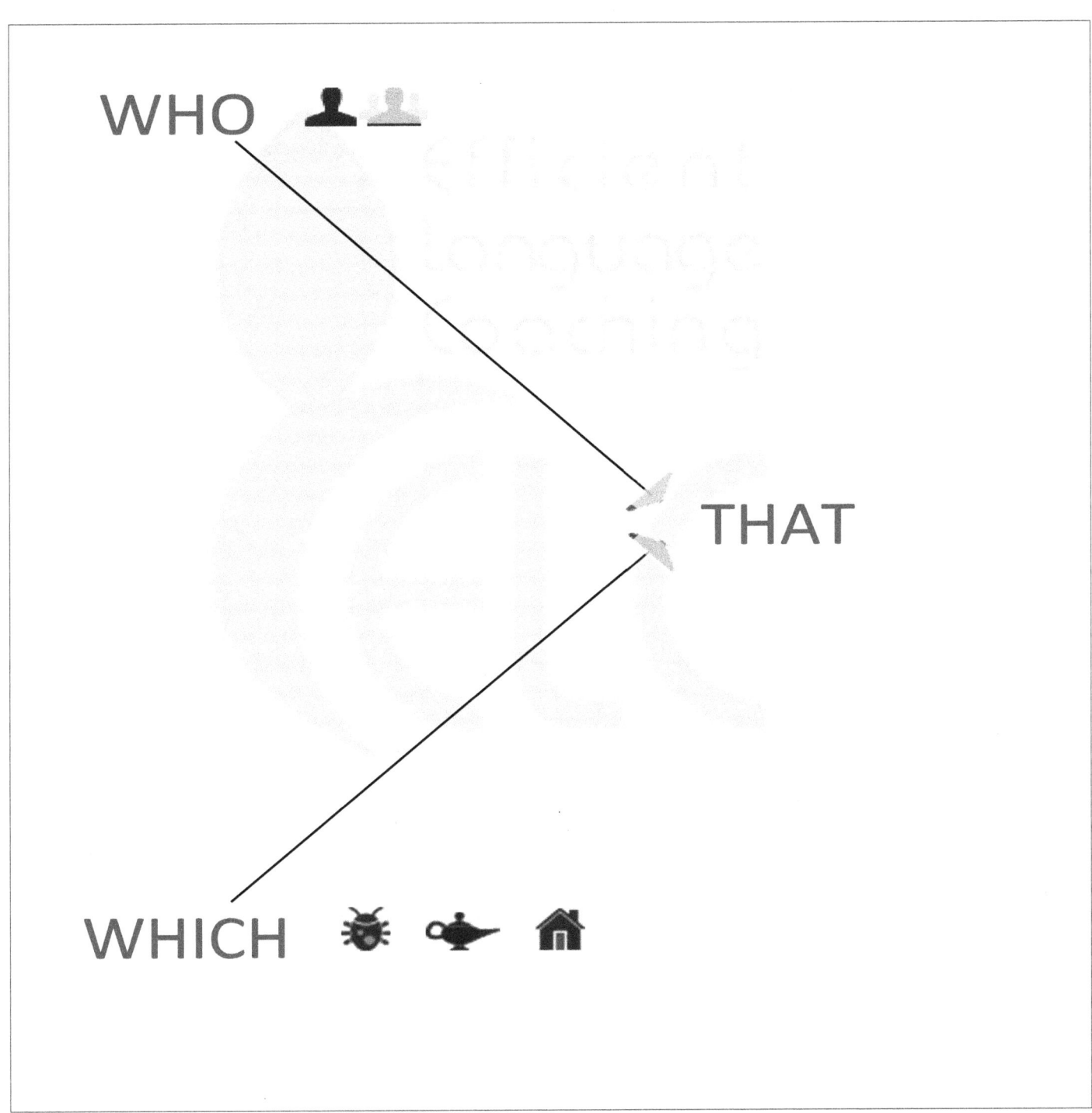

17. PREPOSITION FAMILIES

PREPOSITIONS OF PLACE
- at
- in / inside - out / outside
- into =/ - out of
- on / onto / on top of
- on =/ - off
- under / underneath / beneath
- across / through
- above =/ - below
- over
- among >2 - between =2
- by / beside / near / next to
- along / past
- to / towards =/ from
- in front of / opposite =/ behind
- up =/ down
- round / around

PREPOSITIONS OF TIME
- IN – year / month / season / part of the day (morning, afternoon...)
- ON – day / date / single day
- AT – clock time / meal time / special times (e.g. Easter, Christmas)
- Point of time – BY/FROM/TO/SINCE
- Duration of time – UNTIL/FOR/WHILE/DURING

SUGGESTED CONVERSATION

P - Welcome to our session today. One of your mechanical goals is to work on prepositions and we had scheduled to start this topic today. Is that OK with you?

A - Super. So may I ask you, if we could break the prepositions down and really take them step by step. Firstly, may I ask you, just out of curiosity, what is a preposition for you?

PQ - Can I check if you have them in your language? And are there so many?

A - If we just take a moment to talk about the functions of prepositions, what comes to mind for you?

CL and T - OK, so we could categorise them into time, place, location, direction, spatial relationships and may I also add we can use them to introduce an object.

P - Looking first at the prepositions of time, to start with, we will focus on the IN ON AT, which can get a little confusing. Then we will look at the prepositions which indicate a point in time and then those that indicate duration of time. How does that sound?

PQ and CL - Before we move on, how would you like to create a reminder of what we are going to be covering? So I am hearing you would like to create a visual in the form of tables, super!

A - So, looking at the preposition IN, when do we use this in relation to time?

PQ - Yes absolutely, we use it for years, months and seasons. What would you use in your language?

PQ - OK, that is interesting, you are saying that in Spanish you use the word EN, which sounds very similar to IN! And I am hearing it really is the same as we say "in January" and in Spanish "en enero" - it really is exactly the same - just the preposition and the noun. What about "in 1999", how would you say that in Spanish?

PQ - "En 1999" is once again exactly the same. How do you feel about those examples?

A - Great, now what else can we use IN for?

A - Well done. You are right, we say IN THE MORNING, IN THE AFTERNOON and IN THE EVENING. What about NIGHT?

T - Actually, may I share with you that we can say IN THE NIGHT, but the meaning is different. It means during the night and I would not use this if I just want to point out a reference to nighttime. May I give you an example? "We sleep at night" compared to "He woke up in the night when his dog jumped on the bed."

PQ - Can I check with you, how do you say all those expressions in Spanish?

PQ - That is really interesting, so in Spanish you actually use a different preposition – POR instead of EN. So you say por la tarde, por la mañana and even por la noche. What about the differences in those two sentences, how would you translate those?

(learner offers the following sentences: *Dormimos por la noche* means we sleep at night and *se despertó en la noche cuando su perro salto encima de la cama* means he woke in the night when his dog jumped on the bed!

CL - OK great, so here we can clearly see "in the night" is exactly the same in Spanish and with the same use and "at night" would be using the preposition POR in Spanish. Interesting!

PQ - So how do you feel now about IN? Can we move onto the preposition ON?

A - OK, so looking at ON, when would we use this proposition?

C - Great yes, on concrete days and dates, what examples could you give me?

Yes, such as on Monday or on the 23rd of April, well done!

PQ - How's that in Spanish?

CL - That's interesting. You actually say the day or the date with the article, so "el lunes" or "el 23 de abril" whereas in English we use the preposition ON.

A - We have looked at these two uses, can I check if anything else comes to mind with ON?

T - May I share with you, we could also use it for special days, for example ON Christmas day.
C - What other examples could you give me like that?

Yes, super, on my birthday for example.

P - So far, we have looked at IN and ON, in relation to time, may we move now to AT?

A - When do we use this in relation to time?

PQ - Exactly right, we use it for clock time. How do you say that in Spanish?

CL - Oh, so I am hearing you say A LAS TRES for AT three o'clock, so I am sensing that it is quite similar in sound, but the preposition is actually different, am I right?

A - May I stretch you for some more uses of AT?

PQ - Yes well done, we also use it with meals, AT breakfast, AT lunch, AT dinner. How is that in Spanish?

PQ - OH so that is completely different – you say EN/IN. How could we create alarm bells here for you?

PQ - What could help you remember that?

A - We have looked at the time with AT and also meals, what else could we use it for?

C - May I share this with you, we can also use it for special times, for example, AT Christmas. What other examples could you give me?

Great AT Easter is a lovely example.

P and PQ - Now we have covered IN ON and AT. How are you feeling about those?

P and A - I would like to move into other prepositions of time. In particular, there are certain prepositions that can point to a certain pinpoint in time and others that give the feeling of duration. If we look at the point in time first, what prepositions come to mind for you?

C - Yes, super example, BY tomorrow. How would that be in an example sentence?

A - What other prepositions could point to time? Excellent SINCE 1999.

T - Any others? May I share with you, we could also introduce FROM and TO here as they go from point to point, as an example we could say I work FROM nine to five.

P - So, summing up we have FROM and TO which often go together and also SINCE and BY.

A - Now moving to the ones that give the feeling of duration of time. What comes to mind for you there?

A - UNTIL, yes. How could you use that in a sentence? Super, "we have until next week to leave the house".

A - Any others? Yes, I have lived here FOR ten years, which gives the feeling of a period of time and not a point which would be demonstrated with SINCE 1999.

T - May I share a couple of others that I was thinking of? Have you heard of DURING and WHILE?

PQ - How would they be in Spanish? DURANTE and MIENTRAS.

PQ - So can I ask you, what is the difference between them?

cl- Oh well done! DURING would be followed by a noun, yes! And MIENTRAS by a subject and a verb, yes! Is that the same in Spanish? OH that is interesting, so I am hearing it would be exactly the same in Spanish!

P - OK, well done, we have covered IN ON AT and we have now added FOR and SINCE, FROM and TO, BY and UNTIL.

PQ - How are you feeling with all these prepositions of time?

C - How about we go into a conversation and see if we can use as many as we can...

18. ACTIVE TENSE OVERVIEW

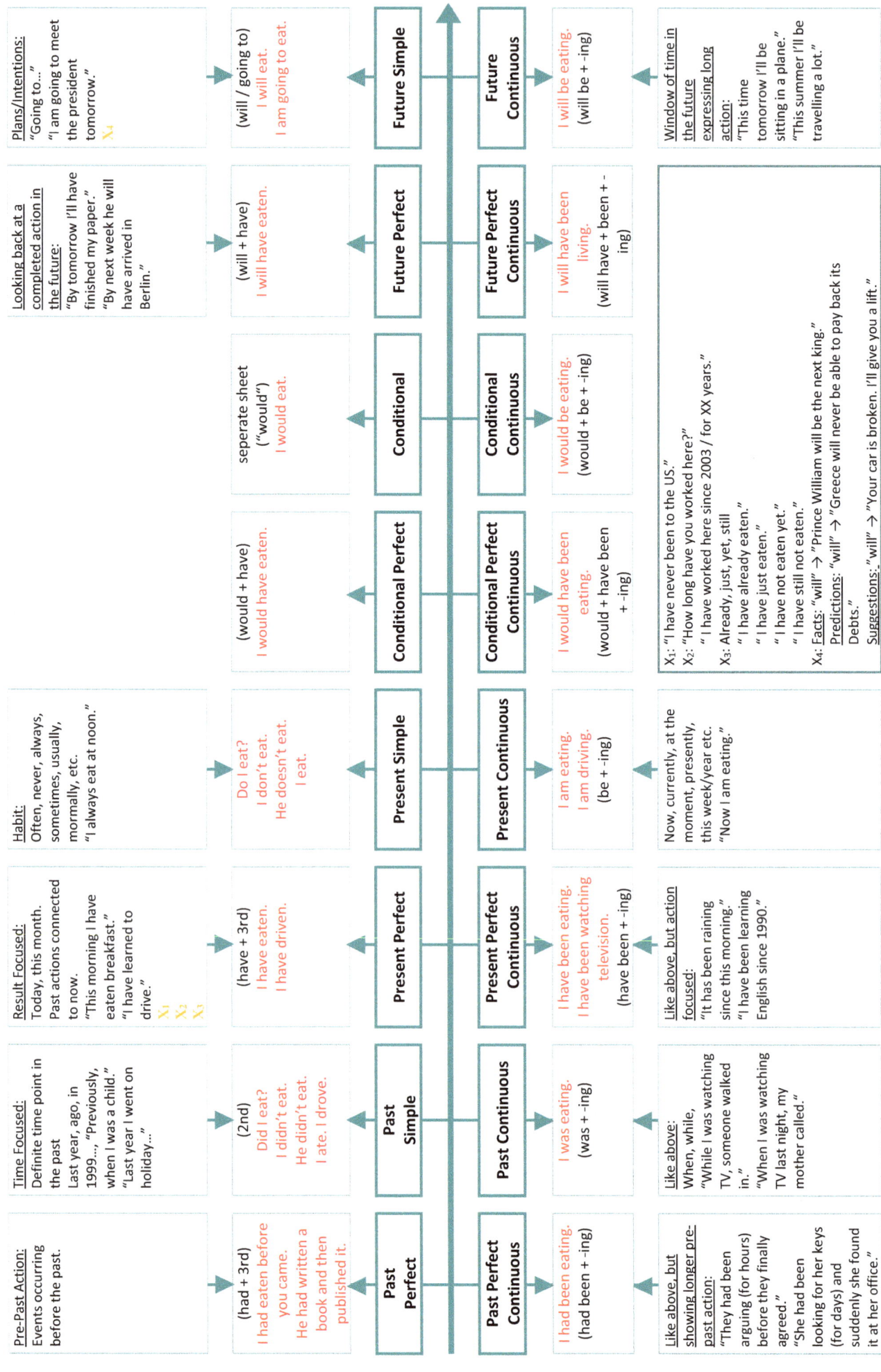

Conditionals

If x, then y.

0 conditional – if + present, then + present – facts and factual situations

If I write a paper, I use a pen.
If it rains, I take an umbrella.

1st conditional – if + present, then + future

If it rains, I will come home.
If I eat too much, I will get fat.

2nd conditional – if + past, then + conditional.

If I won the lottery, I would disappear.
If Germany won the next championship, then Brazil would be sad.
If the EC were to adopt that new MIFID, then every trader would have to become a bank.

3rd conditional – if + past perfect, then conditional perfect.

If I had known, I would not have gone.

If the EC had adopted the right measures, then there would have been better results.

19. PASSIVE TENSE OVERVIEW

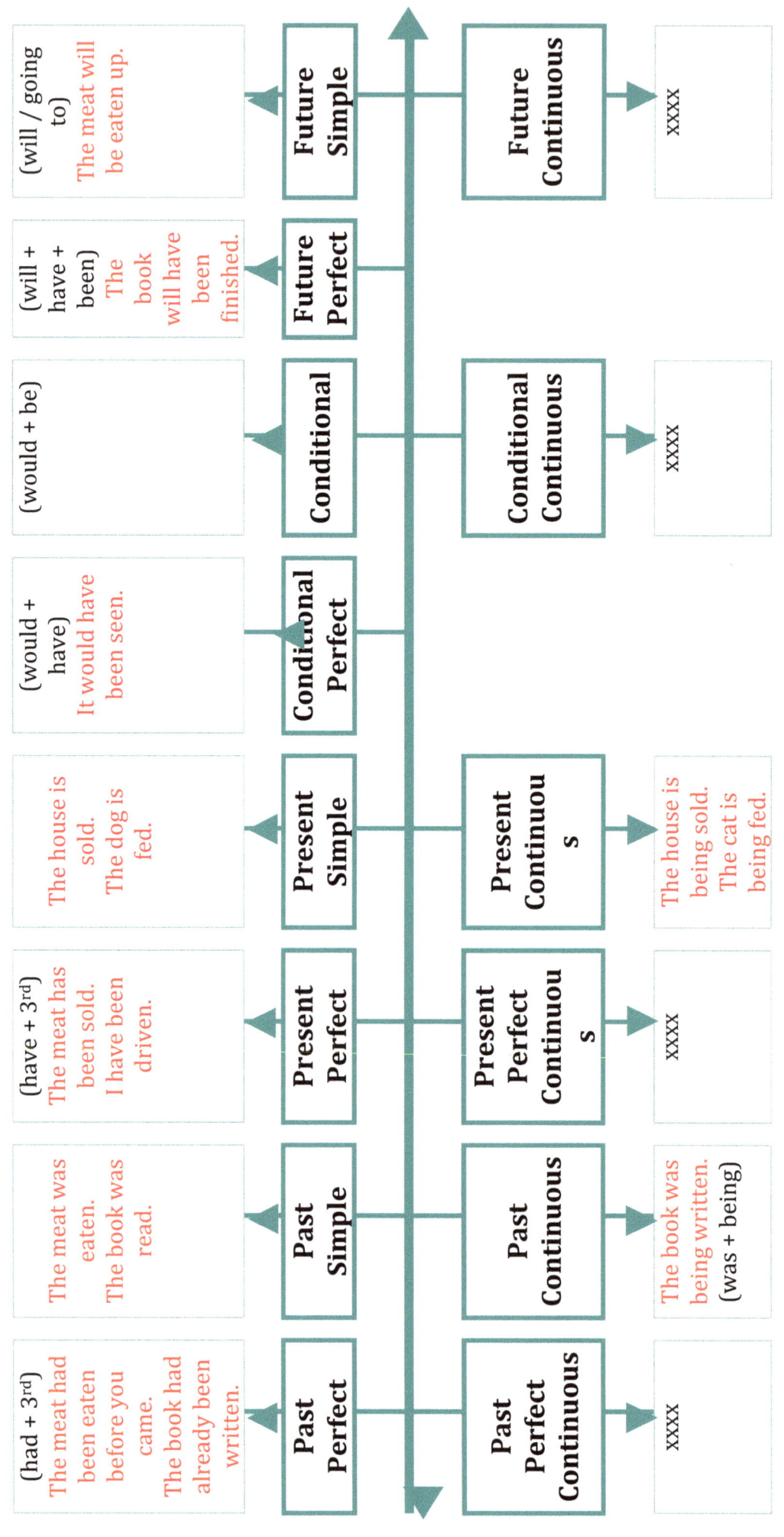

TENSE OVERVIEW

I have to say thank you to one of my clients for this overview of the tenses in this timeline format! About 15 years ago, he asked if we could create an overview and we sat and created this together. I have to admit that at that time, it also helped me to situate the tenses in English and to really get the timeline right in my own mind! Even as a native speaker, I had not got a clear overview of the big picture.

The idea with this visual is that you COCREATE this with your client. If you have a higher level client, you can sit in that space and create together, explaining that the simple and perfect will go on the top and the continuous equivalents along the bottom.

With lower level learners, you could have the visual with the empty boxes and then together, when you actually coach the learner into one of the tenses, you could situate it on the visual and then keep adding the new tenses as you do them. In this way, you help them build the time line in their mind and you also help them build in the understanding of how they relate to other tenses. You could start in the middle with the present tenses and then towards the left go into the past and towards the right into the future and conditional.

It really should be a step by step build up and once you have the active time line completed, you could then ask the learner to create the same style timeline for the passive.

There are many languages which really only have a past, a present and a future, (for example, German, and Polish), so this visual really helps these learners to situate the nuances between the English tenses. I always think that English tenses add "shades of pastel colours" to the major colours PAST PRESENT and FUTURE.

You could even ask the learner to place on the timeline how they would express that particular tense in their language, so they have the equivalent visually placed next to the English.

The most important thing is that you get the coachee really connecting with the different tenses and also how they relate to each other. When going through the tenses with learners, I always recommend to build up the conversation following a pattern: first the formation of that tense, then the uses and break these down into compartmentalised uses and finally what are the trigger words (adverbs of time) indicating you are in that tense. The brain naturally patterns, so this conversation echoes and follows this to assist the brain to do it faster!

20. WHICH TENSE SHOULD I CHOOSE?

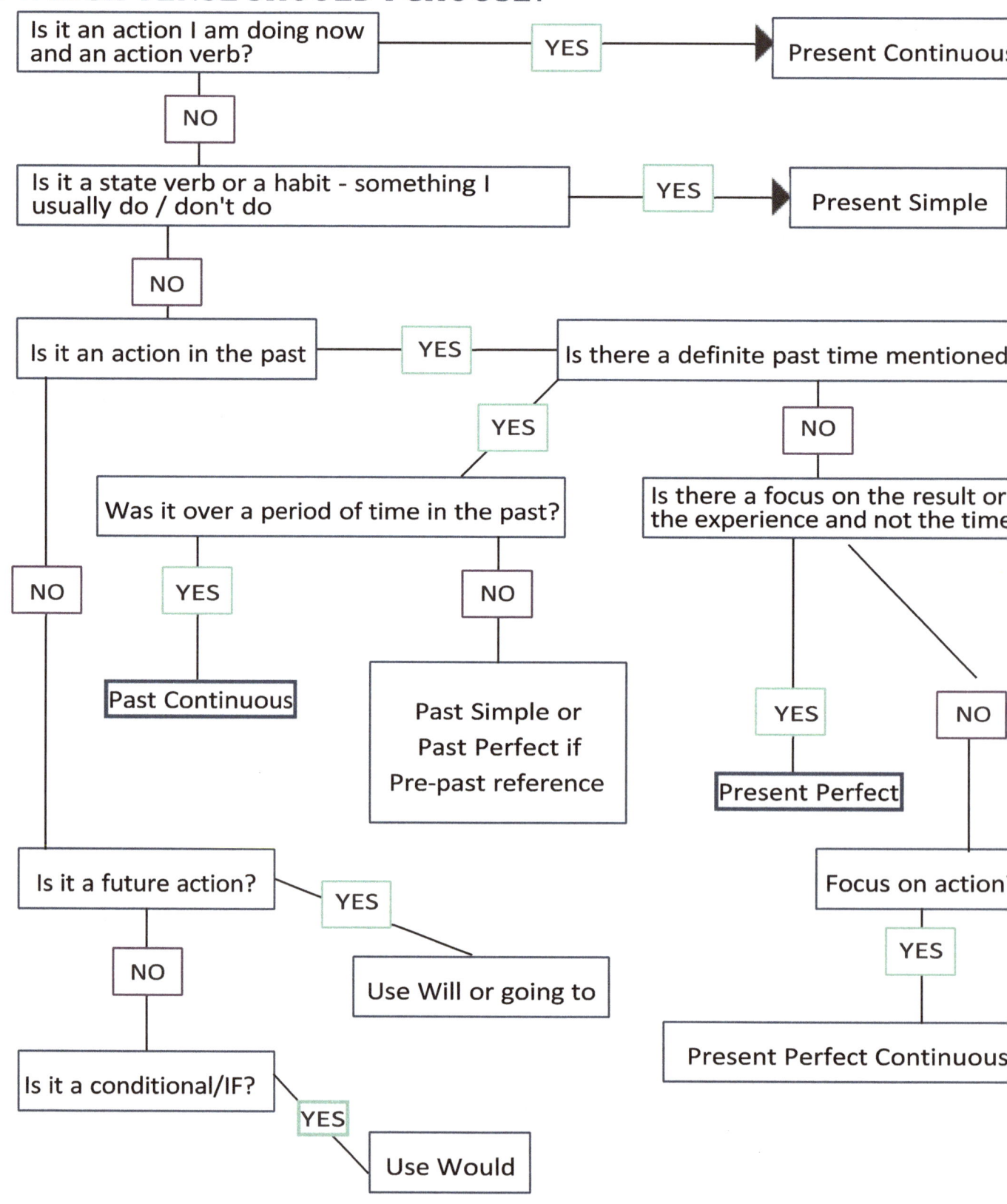

This particular mind-map could be a great way of helping the coachee to discover the reasons for choosing certain tenses in English when we are speaking. If you are working with an advanced learner, it could be useful to really find out where the confusion and problems are and if working with lower levels, it could be used to cocreate this together as the learner touches upon the tenses and keep coming back to add to the mind map ass the learner progresses and advances. The coach would be asking the questions throughout to provoke the creation of the mind map:

How would you feel if we start with the focus on the present – so maybe we can start with the question – "Is it an action that you are doing now?" And maybe we can bring out the YES answer to this side and the NO to go down to another question. With the YES answer, which tense comes up for you then? (Present continuous.)

With the NO answer, we would need to then move to the next question, "Is this something that I usually do or is it a truth/fact?"

Great you have identified that this would be then the present simple, can we indicate that with the YES and then place that tense into the box. Moving now to the NO answer, how about we check then if it is an action in the past? If you think about the past tenses you know, what could be an ideal question here to find out which tense we could bring in next with the YES and NO scenario?

Super, yes! You have mentioned a fixed time in the past. So, we could ask firstly – is it an action in the past – leading to a yes or a no – if we say yes, then we could ask. 'Is there a definite time in the past associated with the action?' What tense in the past highlights definite time references? Yes, the past simple! What if there is a time mentioned but the action happens over a period of time? May I share with you, this would be the past continuous. Can I check if you know this one?

May we put these two onto the mind-map? Now going back to the question whether there is a definite time mentioned, if we answer NO here, then we could move into exploring the present perfect and the present perfect continuous – may I share with you how we could place this on the mind map? We could in fact ask, is the focus on the result or the action? Which do you think is the answer for these questions?

Yes that is right – if the focus is on experience and result, then it is the present perfect and if it is more on the action then it would be the present perfect continuous. How do you feel about those?

Now, we have in fact covered all the past tenses with those questions and answers. How about we come back to the mind map and then if it is not present or past, we would need to look at the future. How could we ask the question here? Yes, is it an action in the future and if it is then we would use either WILL or GOING TO. If it is not a future, what could be the final question? May I add it here at the end? Is it a conditional sentence, then the answer would be to use WOULD.

How do you feel about this journey through the tenses? How would you feel if we look at every step of the way and compare them all with your native language tenses?

21. TRIGGER WORDS FOR TENSES

PRESENT SIMPLE
Always, never, often, not often, seldom

Rarely, sometimes, usually, normally

Every day / each day, regularly, habitually

PRESENT CONTINUOUS
Now, at the moment, at present, currently, nowadays, this week....

This month, today, look! (now), listen! (now)

PAST SIMPLE
Yesterday, last night, last week, three days ago

Formerly, previously, when I was young

PAST CONTINUOUS
When, while, during (the night), as...

At the same time as...

PRESENT PERFECT
Ever, never, just, already, yet, still, this week this month, once / twice / three times etc.

How long? for, since

PRESENT PERFECT CONTINUOUS
How long?

For, since, just

PAST PERFECT
Just, already, by 1960, before

The creation of this visual with the learner could really help to recognise the key adverbial time words that indicate the possible tense. Highlighting these words could help the brain to trigger into the tenses, so they really are key words for the subconscious brain. With an advanced learner, it could be interesting to brainstorm these together with the coachee to create the database of key indicators. With a lower level learner, when exploring every new tense, there should always be reference to these trigger words, so he/she learns it together with those triggers. You could also start to create the boxes and then keep adding ass the new triggers come out.

(N.B : there may be some words that can be used for various tenses and you may need to highlight these to the learner)

22. TENSE BUILDERS

SIMPLE	DO DID	Present Past
PERFECT	HAVE HAD	Present Past Future Conditional
CONTINUOUS	BE WAS - WERE	Present Past Present Perfect Past Perfect Future Future Perfect Conditional Conditional Perfect
PASSIVE	BE	All Tenses

This is a super visual to cocreate with the learner to really ensure that the learner understands the "helper" verbs for the formation of each tense. There could be that constant reference to the native language tenses to see how they create the tenses, if they exist in their native language.

This also helps the learner to really clarify the types of tenses and how the SIMPLE tenses use DO/DID – the perfect tenses use HAVE and HAS/HAD – the continuous tenses use BE/WAS-WERE and the passive uses BE.

The interesting thing is that you can then really check with the coachee how to create "mixes" and really get the coachee playing with combinations – for example

- PRESENT PERFECT CONTINUOUS will include both HAVE and BE in some way - I have been eating
- PRESENT PERFECT PASSIVE includes HAVE and BE - The bone has been eaten
- PASSIVE PRESENT CONTINUOUS includes BE twice - The bone is rapidly being eaten

23. PRESENT SIMPLE

The next mind-map takes a learner through the options relating to the formation of the PRESENT SIMPLE and in particular when talking about habits and routines.

It is designed to help a learner to consolidate what needs to be remembered when making a positive statement (especially the "s" in third person), when asking the question (DO and DOES) and when forming a negative statement (DO NOT and DOES NOT). The contracted forms of the latter could also be explored DON'T and DOESN'T.

It is a relatively straightforward visual to re-create with the learner through signposting, asking the right questions and really seeing if the coachee him/herself could map this out.

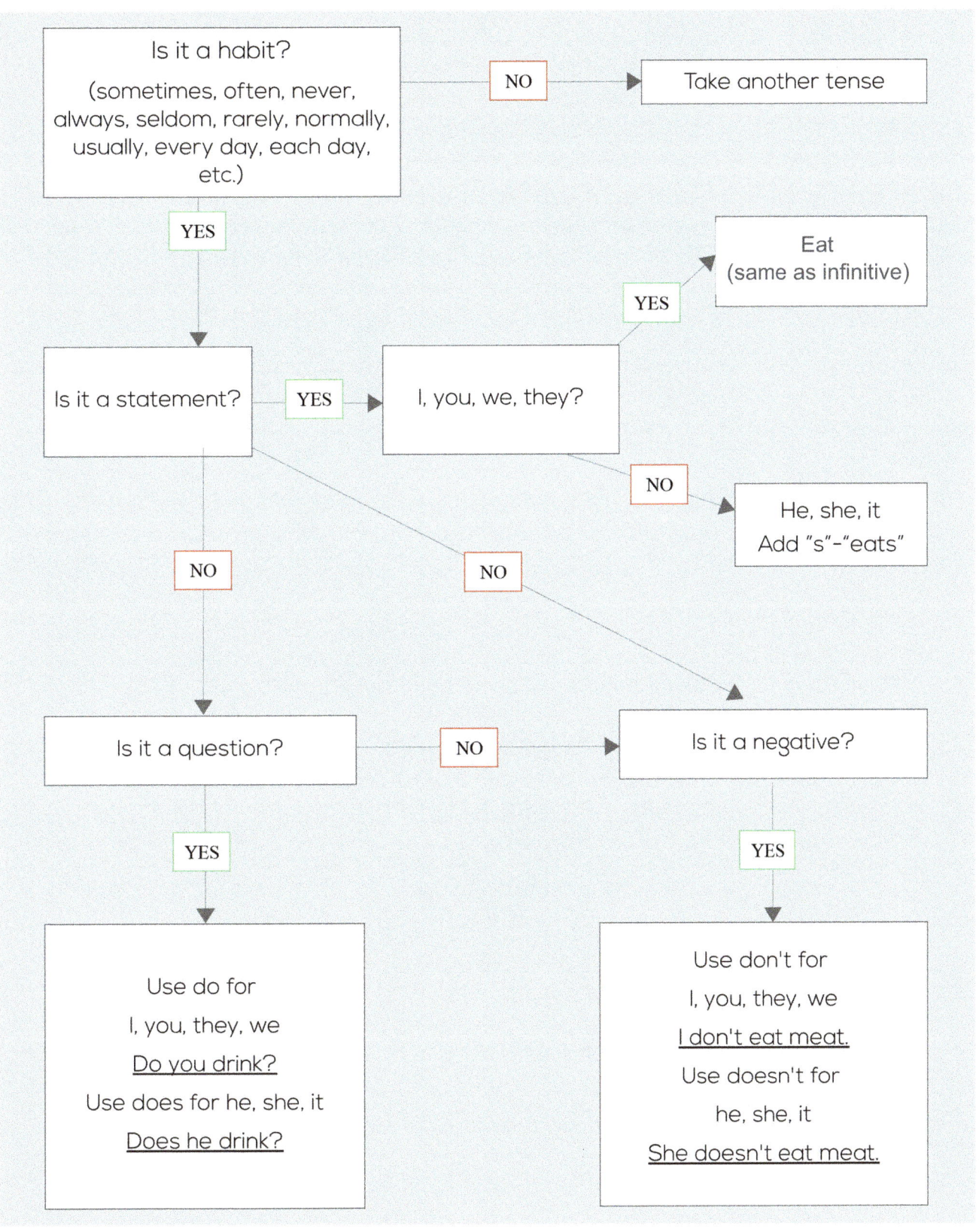

24. STATE VERBS GROUPS (Verbs of "being" not "action verbs")

The next two pictures are great visuals to create categories for the state verbs. I always say you can help the learner by getting them into the BRAIN, HEART, PROPERTY, CONTAINER and EXISTENCE groups. You may find that you could classify some verbs in either the BRAIN or the EXISTENCE groups and it could be interesting to see where your learner would place the verbs, to ensure that they are the ones connecting with the categories.

For Spanish and Italian natives learning English it could also be interesting to see if these state verbs in their own languages are also not used in the continuous form – for example in Spanish you would never say "estoy sabiendo" – "I am knowing" - exactly the same as in English.

The first picture has five different categories and the second has only three. You might want to check in with the learner and ask which would be more helpful for him/her to recognise and learn them.

Example parts of the conversation could be:

Today, we said we would look at the difference between what we call action verbs and state verbs. May I check with you how you feel about the difference between these two?

How about in your language, do you separate out these two types of verbs?

We will start to see how we could group these in English – I propose that we create five different groups. We will call these the BRAIN, HEART, CONTAINER, EXISTENCE, and PROPERTY groups. How do they sound?

If we take the BRAIN group first, we are looking for verbs that really reflect "brain states". Could we brainstorm these together? What comes to mind when you think of this category?

Super, yes, to know. Anything else? Yes great, to believe, to understand, comprehend – well done! May I add some more?

(And in this way, the conversation would continue, interacting with the coachee and building up the lists within each category.)

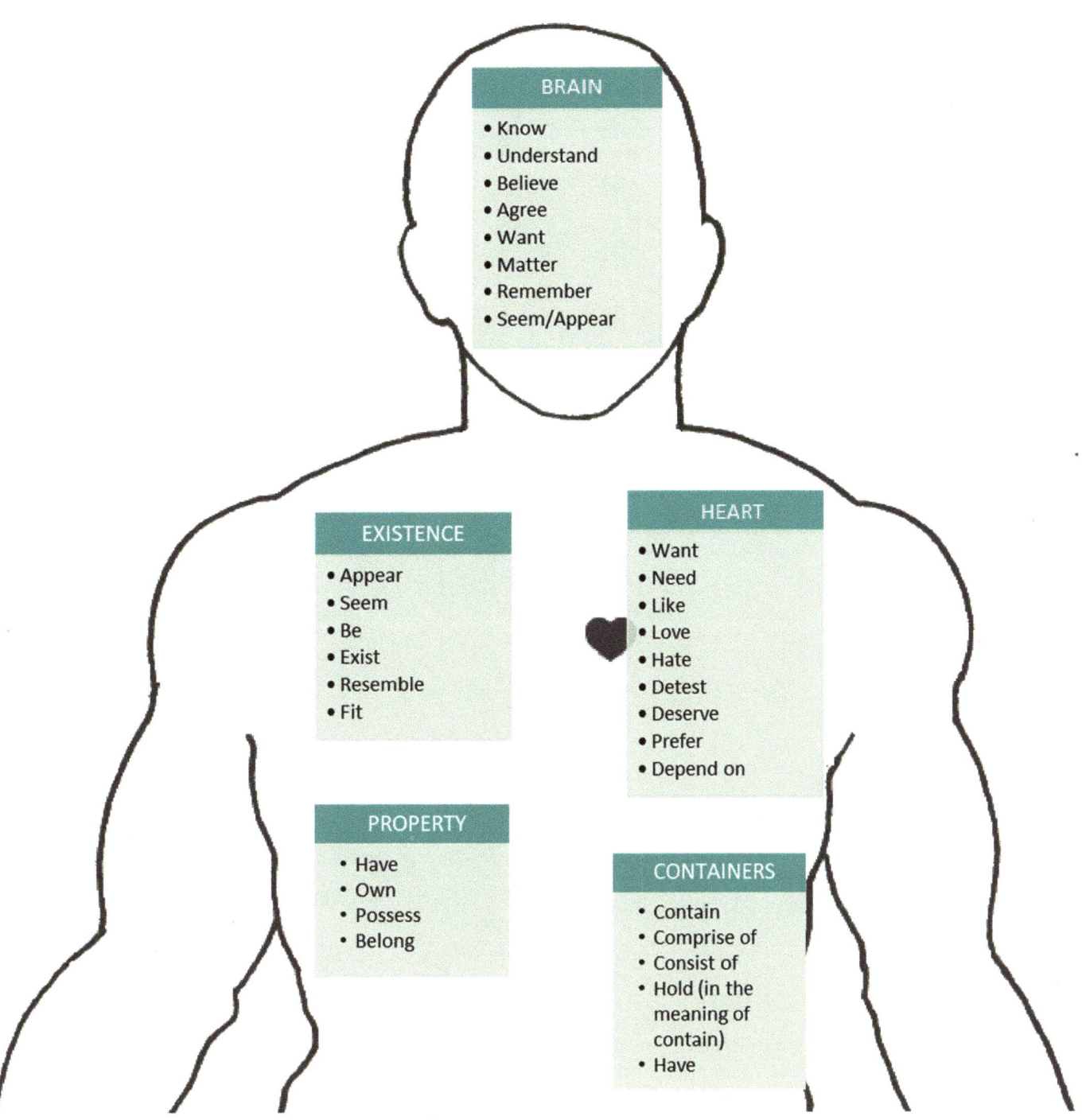

25. STATE VERBS (Verbs of "being" and not "action verbs")

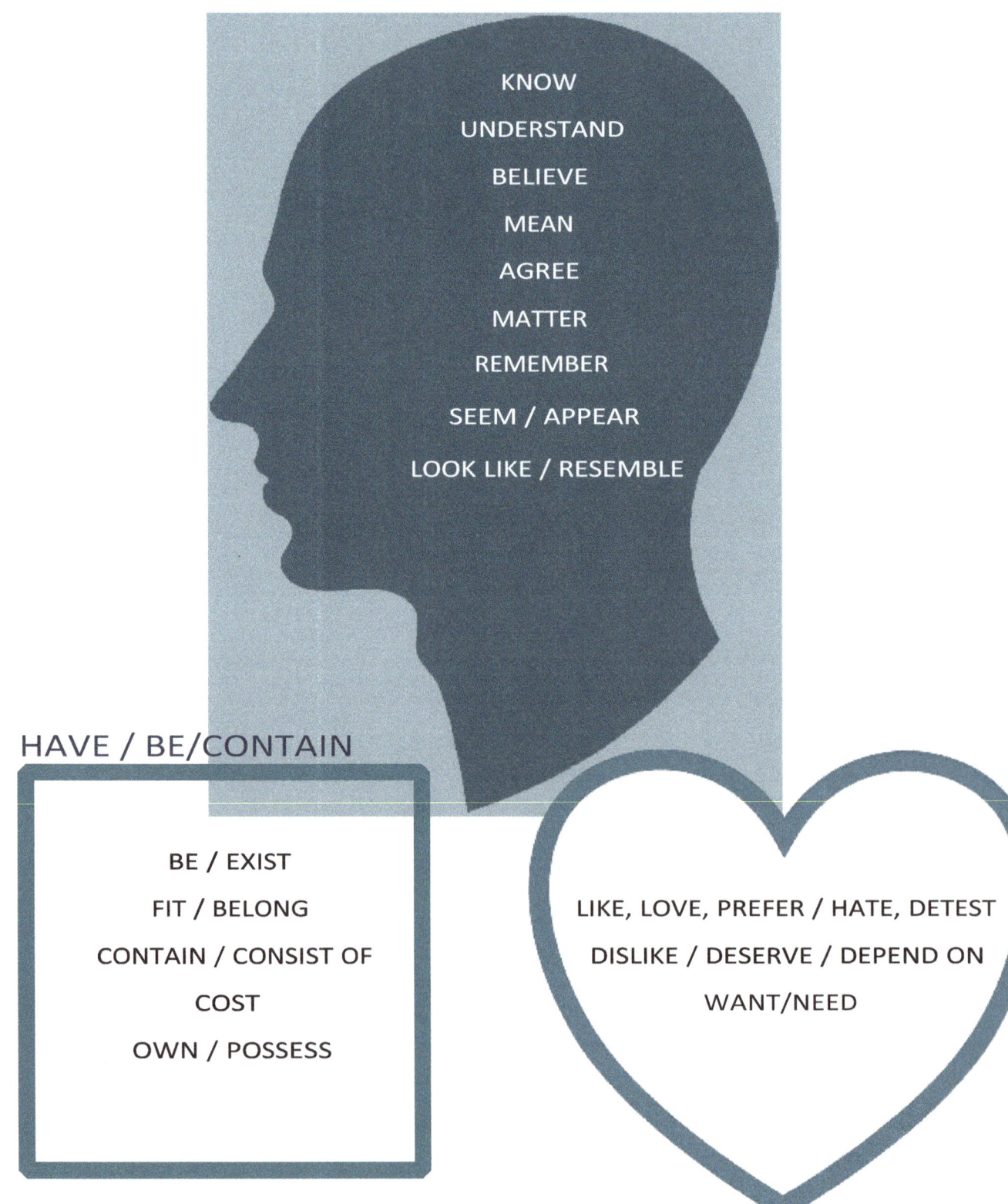

26. PRESENT SIMPLE or PRESENT CONTINUOUS

This is an example of creating the flow together with the coachee to demonstrate the difference between the present simple and the present continuous. This will be really useful for those native speakers who have no concept of the present continuous in their mind, as this tense does not exist in their mother tongue. By asking the right questions we can help the brain develop the right way of thinking and the right logic to determine which present tense to use.

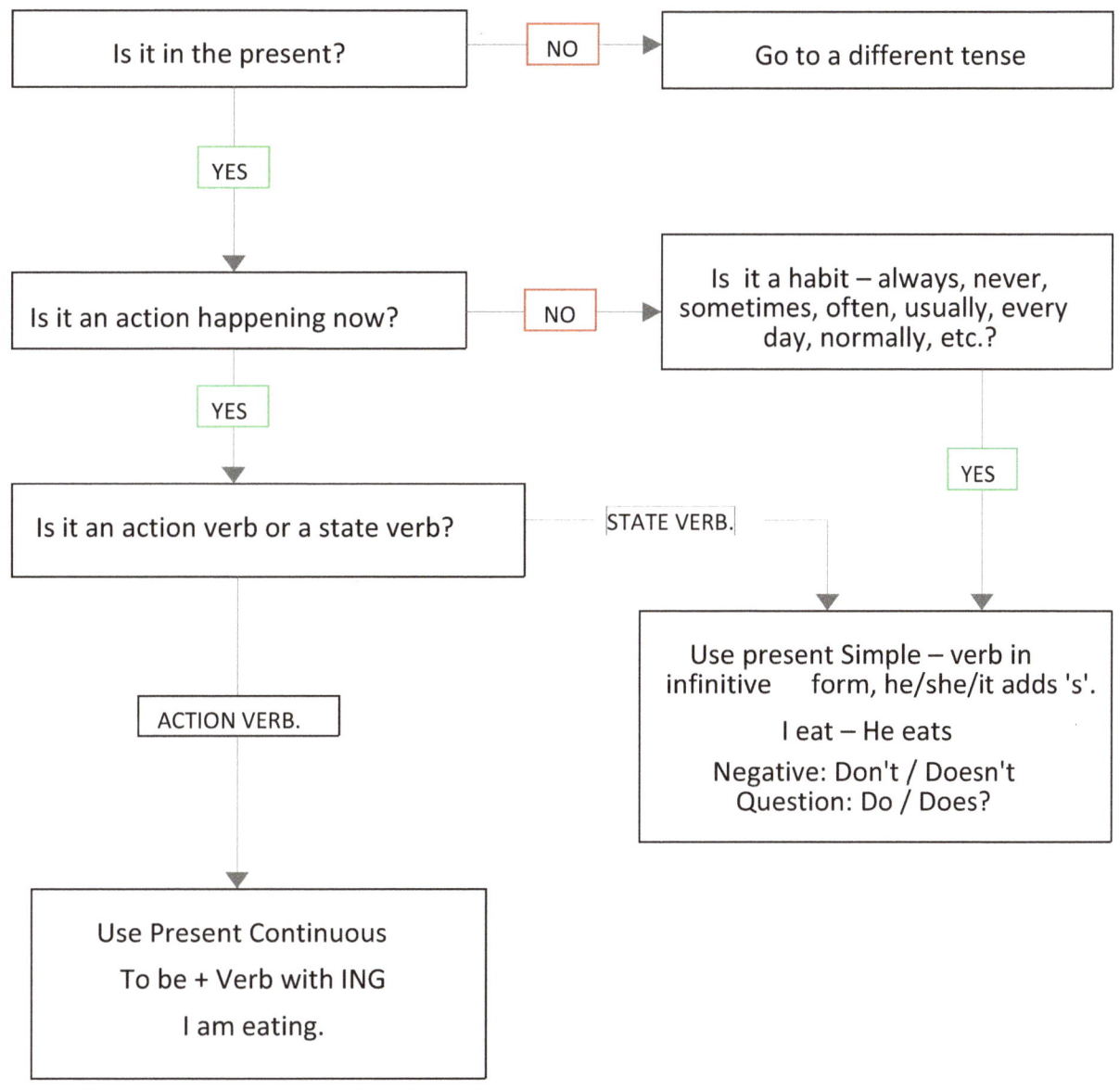

27. PRESENT PERFECT

One of the major difficulties when learning the present perfect in English is to understand the different uses. In many languages the present perfect does not even exist, so it is really important to help the learner to compartmentalise when it can be used. This visual can be created according to how the learner would like it, I have created it like a spider mind map with the main idea in the middle and then lines and boxes that branch out to highlight the different uses.

It would also be useful to get the learner to really connect with the "trigger words" for each use (highlighted in yellow on the diagram), because these will help the brain to recognise the scenarios and use the present perfect.

Another key point in the compartmentalisation is the separate "box" for "how long, for and since". There is a very significant reason for this, as in most languages the present tense would be used. For this reason, it is important for the learner to flag this up, as the natural tendency, due to native interference, will always be to go into the present – how long do you live here? Instead of, how long have you lived here? I really recommend to take the learner through this particular part by referring to native. For example:

"Now, moving to the next use of the present perfect. May I say that we use it with the question "how long" and the answers to this with "for and since".

Could you give me any examples of this use?

How would you say this in your native language?"

So, I am hearing that you would use the present tense here. May I share with you that in English, this would definitely be the present perfect, so we would need you to really pay attention to this, as the natural tendency for you would be to ask or answer using the present.

How can I help you remember this?

How about we go into a conversation and we try and use how long, together with for and since, to really get you used to this…

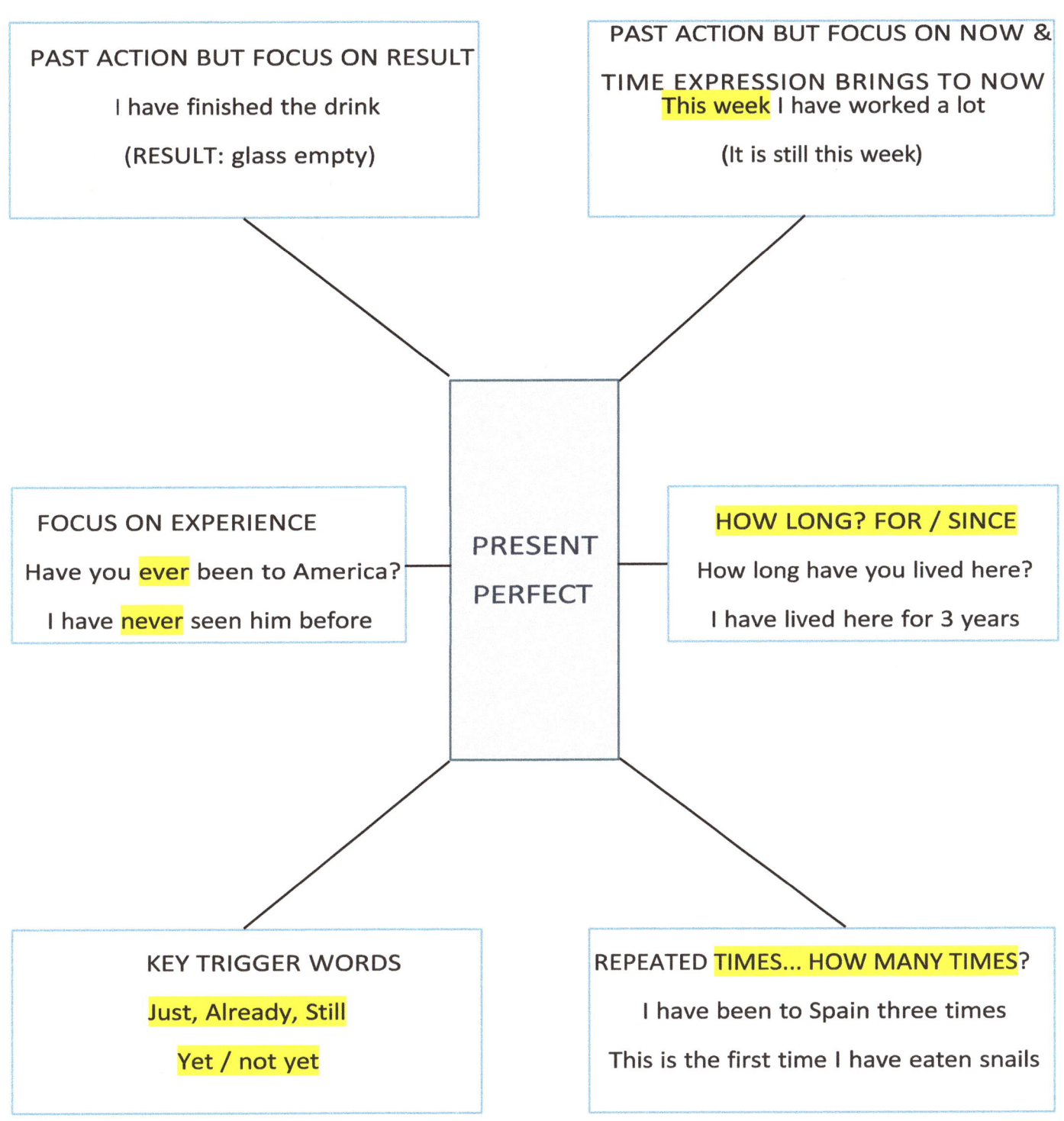

28. PAST SIMPLE OR PRESENT PERFECT

This is another example of creating the flow together with the coachee to demonstrate the difference between the past simple and the present perfect. By asking the right questions we can help the brain to develop the right logic to determine when to use the present perfect or the past simple.

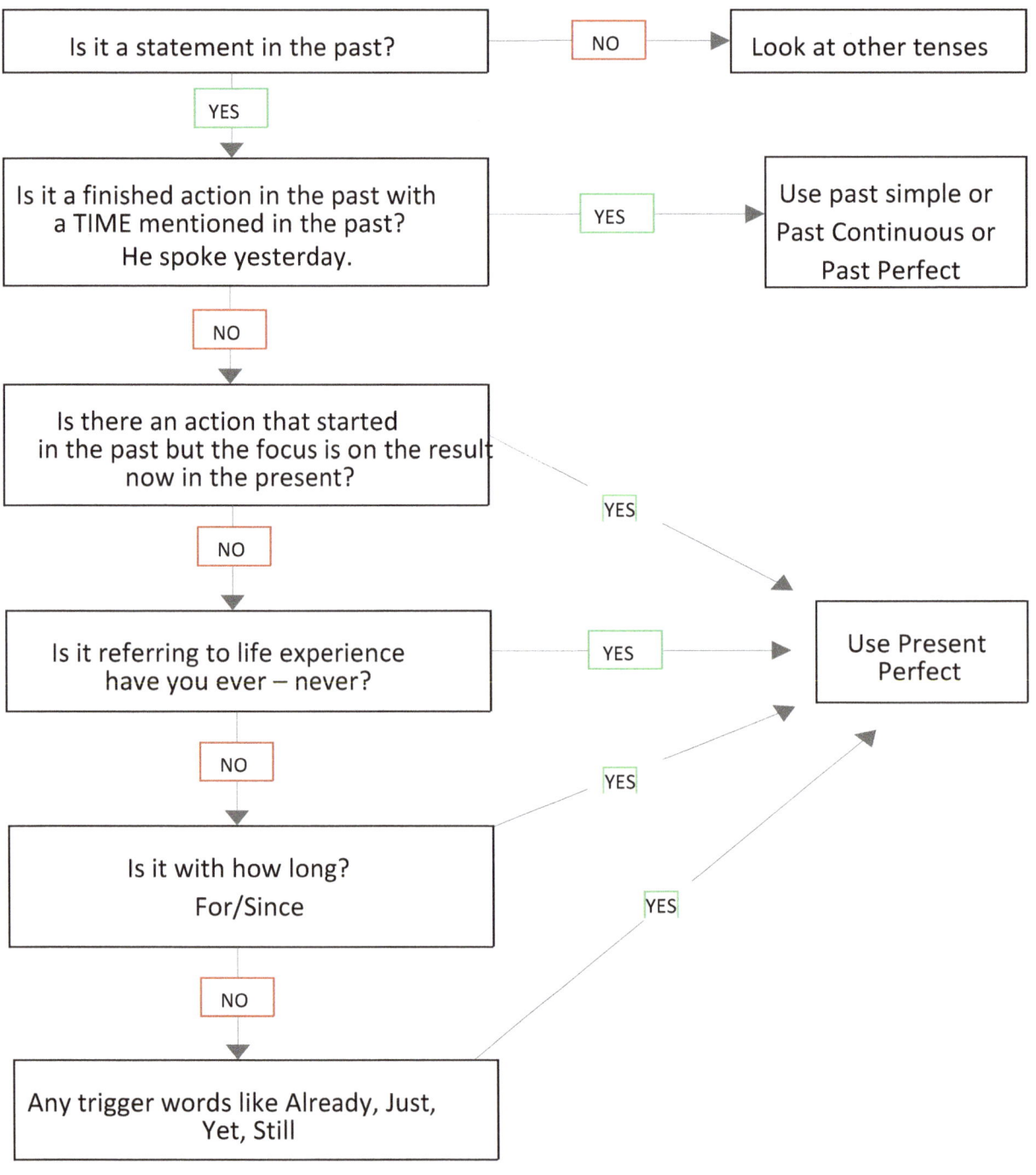

29. IRREGULAR VERB FAMILIES – Cocreate groups with the learner´s most used irregular verbs

Before I introduce this, I would like to confess that when I was teaching fifteen to twenty years ago, I would do multitude of copies of the irregular verb list and then give these to my learners to go through and learn. Sometimes I would go through the list with them and we would highlight the most useful or the most used, so that they could really focus on those, but other times I would just give them the list to look through by themselves! Now, I would strongly suggest that you sit and cocreate the "useful irregular verb list" with the learner and at the same time categorise them into "irregular verb families" and at the same time make it fun and curious for the learner. You may decide to create the families in a different way – however you do this, the most important is that you help the learner to connect easily and quickly with the irregular endings, as most learners find this quite traumatic! You could also highlight to learners that the regular past and past participle ending -ED actually traces back to Latin, but the irregular verbs come from Proto-Germanic and there are many similarities with the German verbs.

For example:

singen-sang-gesungen   sing-sang-sung

bringen brachte gebracht   bring-brought-brought

I recommend taking your learner through this step by step. Whether you are introducing the verbs for the first time or even refreshing and checking on knowledge and trying to build up new vocabulary, breaking the topic into various families will calm the learner and bring more certainty.

Example conversation

Welcome to the session today and we had scheduled to start the topic of the irregular verbs in English today. How do you feel about that?

Maybe I can give you a little preview of how we could do this. I propose introducing the verbs in patterns, because we can really bring in six different types of patterns for these verbs. How does that sound?

By the way, do you have irregular verbs in your language? Out of curiosity, what makes them irregular?

I see! Well, let me introduce you to this topic, by saying we will be looking at six groups. Starting with the first group. May I say this is the easiest group because nothing changes, for example the verb "to put" stays the same in the past and also the past participle. So, the pattern is put-put-put.

How about you give me an example of a sentence using this verb in the present and then another one in the past? (He puts the vase on the dining room table when he has guests but yesterday he put the vase in the kitchen.)

Well done! Now, can I ask you what other verbs do you know follow this same pattern? Yes, well done! Cut is exactly the same. How about we create a list of these?

Can I bring some more to the list?

1. Verb + Past Simple + Past Participle the same

CUT   CUT   CUT
PUT   PUT   PUT

Other verbs in this family: cost, fit, hit, hurt, let, quit, read (with pronunciation change), set

OK, we have the first group. Moving now to the next group. We could call this group, the ones with both the second and third column the same, so instead of all three the same, now we have the infinitive first but then the second and third do not change. If I can give you an example, to find then goes to found, found.

How do you feel about that one?

May I ask if you can think of any others that follow this pattern?

Great yes, win and sit are exactly the same pattern. Can I bring some more into the list?

2. Past Simple and Past Participle the same

FIND   FOUND   FOUND
SIT   SAT   SAT
WIN   WON   WON

Other verbs in this family: get, hear, hold, meet, pay, say, sell, stand, tell, understand

OK, so we now have the first group with all three the same and the second group where two and three are the same. Moving now to the next group and I have to say this is my favourite group, because the pattern sounds funny! We could call this group, the SING SANG SUNG group where the vowel changes in each part and the pattern is I to A to U. If I can give you another example, swim swam swum.

May I give you another verb and you try it out? How about to drink, how would that go?

Yes, super, drink drank drunk. Now shall we try and get some more onto the list? What comes to mind for you?

3. I/u , then a, then u

SING	SANG	SUNG
BEGIN	BEGAN	BEGUN
DRINK	DRANK	DRUNK

Other verbs in this family: swim, ring, run, sink, spring

OK, so we have the first three groups. How about we go into a conversation talking about things in the past and we try and use as many of the verbs on our lists as possible?

Moving now to the next group. You could in fact say that this group is like Group 2, but the one pattern I would like to highlight here is that the second and third endings both have a T. For example, the verbs dream and build, form the past and participle dreamt and built.
May I ask if you can think of any others that follow this pattern?

4. Verb, then t and t

BEND	BENT	BENT
BUILD	BUILT	BUILT

Other verbs in this family: dream, feel, send, sleep, keep, learn, lose, mean

How are you feeling at this point? May I check if you would like us to continue with the final two groups or if you would prefer that we stick with the first four and practise these before moving on?

Can I just check that you are OK to just recap on the first four and then go on? So, the first group was the easy one which stays the same; the second has two and three the same; the third are the funny sing sang sung group and the fourth has a T in position two and three. How are you feeling with those?

Now looking at the next group, we have a slightly different pattern here with an N in position 3. For example, know, knew, known or grow, grew, grown or break, broke, broken. Can I check if you know of any more that follow this pattern?
Great yes, well done, speak, spoke spoken and also eat, ate eaten. Shall we create a list here and brainstorm some more together?

5. With an "n" ending the participle

CHOOSE	CHOSE	CHOSEN
BREAK	BROKE	BROKEN
DRIVE	DROVE	DRIVEN

Other verbs in this family: eat, fall, fly, forget, give, know, see, show, speak, take, write

Finally, I would like to introduce the last group. We could call this group, the OUGHT or AUGHT group as both the second and third column take that ending. If I can give you an example, bring, brought, brought.

How do you feel about that one?

May I ask if you can think of any others that follow this pattern? Yes, great, catch changes to caught caught! May I ask you if you know about teach? Well done, yes, it is the same as catch!

6. OUGHT/AUGHT

BRING	BROUGHT	BROUGHT
BUY	BOUGHT	BOUGHT
TEACH	TAUGHT	TAUGHT
THINK	THOUGHT	THOUGHT

Other verbs in this family: fight, catch

So, we really have explored the different groups and created six different groups with different patterns. How are you feeling about them all? Can I check if there is anything you would like to ask?

How can I help you remember them?

May we move into some more conversation now and practice them as much as we can?

30. FUTURE TENSES (simplifying the future – bearing in mind that there is a lot of interplay between will and going to and different interpretations of the uses, in particular with emphatic statements!)

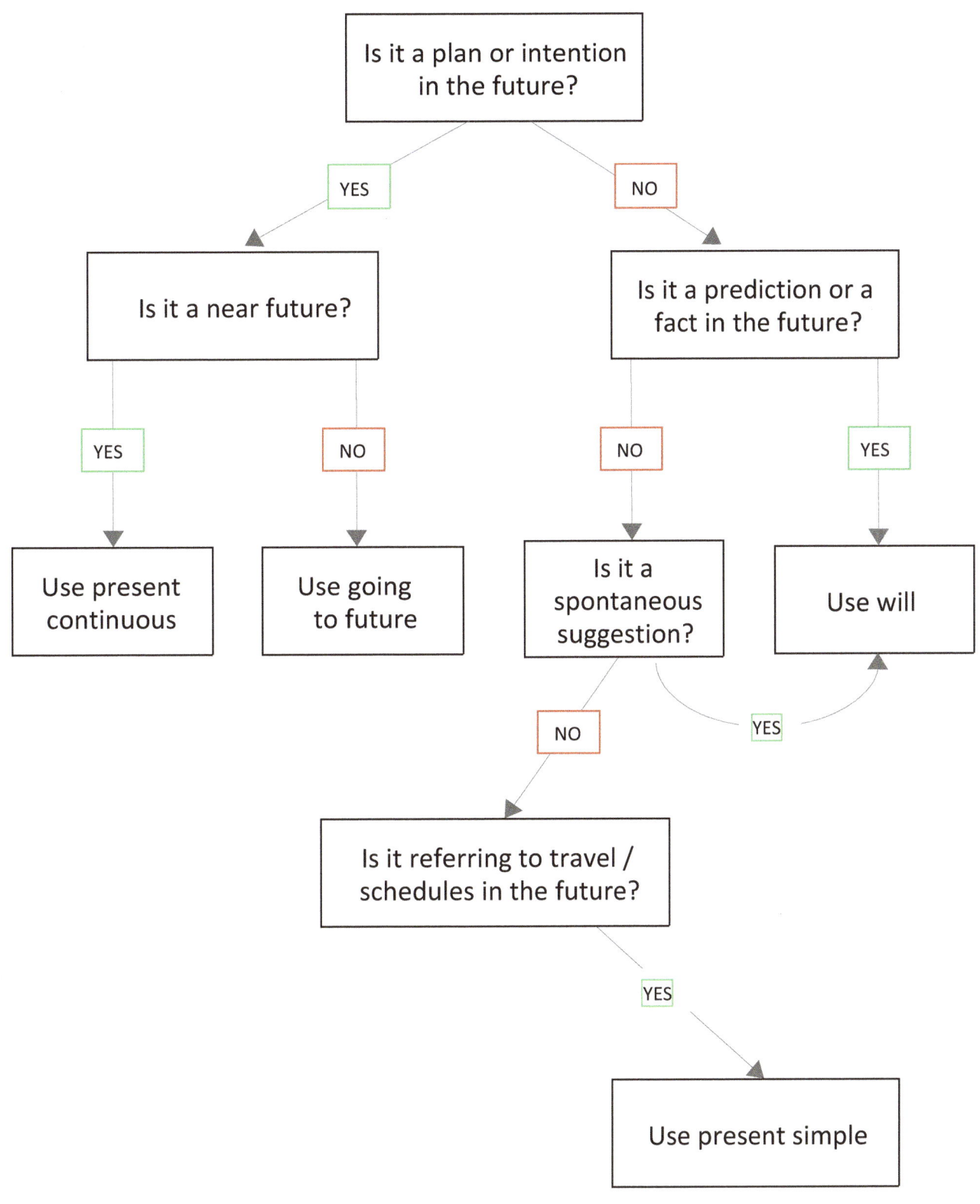

31. CONDITIONALS AS MATHEMATICAL EQUATIONS

This table is ideal for engineers, mathematicians and logical thinkers.

	If x	Then y
0 Conditional	Present tense	(then) present tense
1st Conditional	Present tense	(then) future tense
2nd Conditional	Past tense	(then) conditional
3rd Conditional	Past perfect	(then) conditional perfect

This visual is really, really useful for logically minded learners. I have found that it works extremely well with people who work with mathematics or physics or people who love to work with systematic approaches. I recommend giving the learner the equation to start with "If X, then Y" and from there create the table for each conditional. You could ask the learner the tenses for each one and even ask them to compare it to their native language. I have discovered that in most languages, the zero conditional is nearly always "present and present" so this beautifully corresponds to the English. At each stage you could ask the learner for examples, so the learner can relate and use each one.

Once you have created the table, for more advanced learners, you can then use this to "play" with combinations for mixed conditionals. You could even get the learner to draw the lines, where mixed conditionals could be possible. This will assist the learner to come quickly into the possibilities of mixing them and also explore what works and what does not work.

For example, "If he goes, I would be really happy." (1st plus 2nd.)

32. REPORTED SPEECH - TENSE JUMPS

ONE STEP BACK...

Present Simple	➡	Past Simple
Present Continuous	➡	Past Continuous
Present Perfect	➡	Past Perfect
Present Perfect Continuous	➡	Past Perfect Continuous
Past Simple	➡	Past Perfect
Past Continuous	➡	Past Perfect Continuous
Past Perfect	➡	Past Perfect
Future	➡	Conditional
Future Continuous	➡	Conditional Continuous
Can	➡	Could
Shall / Should	➡	Should
May	➡	Might
Must	➡	Had to

This visual can be used together with the visual earlier in this book numbered 18 which you created with the learner, setting out the big picture for all the tenses in English (the Active Tense Overview). By using that visual, it will be easy to demonstrate the tense jumps, maybe with arrows pointing to the one step backwards.

In the creation of this table, the most important thing is that the learner understands that it will depend on the type (simple, perfect, continuous) when going from present to past – for each swill step back to the next simple in the past – present simple to past simple, present continuous to past continuous, present perfect to past perfect. However, all the past tenses will all go to the final step which will be past perfect or past perfect continuous. The futures step back to conditionals and also modals can be explored to see how they change.

In addition, there could be a conversation around adverbs of time and how they would change to reflect that reporting mode. (I had ice cream today – she said she had had ice cream that day.)

Using the PACT PQC

If the learner is an advanced learner, you would be using the P for placement and signposting and then the A to assess what the learner already knows and see if the learner really can create this big picture with the help of your guidance and stimulation. Wherever you need to, you would then bring in the T to teach/transfer new knowledge if the learner does not know something and as much as possible the PQ to provoke the connections and associations between native and target languages. There could be a lot of C (conversation) to practise reporting back and getting the learner to switch from direct to reported speech.

If you have a lower level learner who is coming into this topic for the first time, I would suggest that you try and springboard the learner from the native and really get the native to notice the verb patterns in the mother tongue and then discover the similarities or differences with English.

33. VERB + Verb in To INFINITIVE   or   VERB + Verb ending in ING

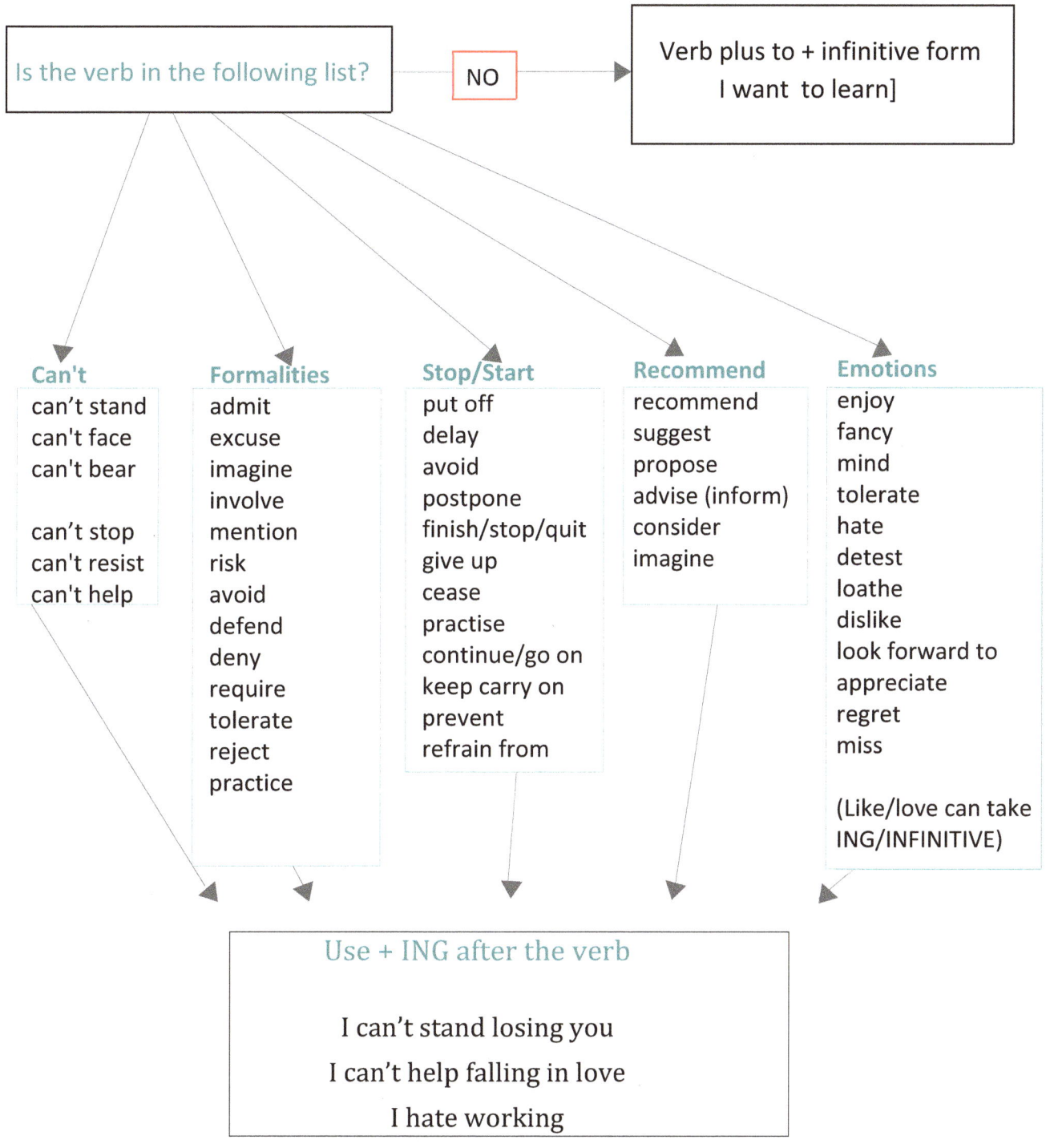

This visual really helps learners to categorise and compartmentalise verbs that are followed by a second verb with an ING ending. You can really explore how the normal pattern in English, when you have two verbs one after the other, is the first verb followed by the "to and infinitive form of the second verb" – for example "I want to eat", "I live to dance" "I work to earn money to travel".

You can assist the learner to really create categories and brainstorm them together – I call them the following categories.

- Can´t
- Formalities
- Stop/start
- Recommenders
- Emotions

In most languages, the natural pattern when two verbs come together is the first followed by the second in infinitive. There could be an introduction to this conversation by really highlighting how the native pattern is and explaining that some verbs in English are different and that this creation of the visual will help to classify these verbs to facilitate recognition of them by the learner.

After this introduction :

How would you feel if we create different boxes and classify them and then brainstorm all the verbs we could think of that could come into these boxes?

So, may I give you the first category – I would like to call them the CAN´T category and these are expressions that normally mean two things. Either I cannot stop doing something or I cannot stand (do not like) doing something. Can I check if you have heard these expressions before? How do you say them in your native language?

Looking at the first one – cannot stop doing – what other expressions do you know with the same meaning? Great yes, "I cannot help doing that" – any other way to express that? May I add we could also say "I cannot resist doing something". How about using all of these with some other examples?

Now let us move into the "cannot stand" – what other expressions do you know here? Well done! I cannot face and I cannot bear – may I ask you for some examples of these as well?

You could then conduct a similar conversation with each category, brainstorming and adding to the list and interacting with the learner all the way, asking for examples and more verbs if they know them, if not, then you would ask permission to introduce the new verbs and ask the learner to create examples with the new verbs.

There may be times where you could get the learner into a themed conversation to practise them. For example, there could be a murder mystery topic for the second category regarding formalities or setting agendas and meetings for the third category. The learner could set the theme and then you improvise with the conversation.

34. ING or TO?

This visual follows on from the previous one and will help learners to recognise the verbs that could actually be followed either by the to plus infinitive or by the verb with the ING ending. However, with a different meaning.

The most important thing is that the learner can once again categorise them and understand the difference. The first three verbs, remember, forget and regret actually follow the same pattern and then go on and stop follow another pattern.

The first ones all relate to time by either referring to something before doing it or referring to it after having done it. Remember/forget/regret plus to and infinitive verb afterwards give the meaning of something in the future – I must remember to call, I should not forget to call, I regret to tell you… whereas with the ING after, the reference is to something in the past. I regret saying that, I remember doing it, I forgot about writing that.

You can assist the learner to create different examples and also explore what differences there would be in their native language when saying both types of sentences. For example, in Spanish, the difference would lie in the choice of tenses after "remember" – so remembering something already done would be followed by a present perfect tense, whereas to remember to do something would be followed by an infinitive.

I remember doing that	recuerdo haber hecho eso
I must remember to do that	debo recordar hacer eso

There could be a coaching conversation to create the step by step build up of this visual, starting the pattern with the first verb remember and then getting the learner to pattern out the next ones. You could then ask the coachee to move into a conversation to practise them all. Key questions like:

What can you remember doing as a child at weekends?

What can you never forget doing?

What do you regret doing?

This coming week, what must you remember to do?

And what should you not forget to do?

Is there anything that you would regret to inform me?

When exploring go on and stop – the highlighted difference is either referring to the same action or actually referring to a new action. The interesting thing in Spanish is that there would be different verbs for each sentence.

He stopped to smoke (he stopped what he was doing to then smoke) (se detuvó a fumar.)

He stopped smoking (he actually stopped smoking which could mean he put the cigarette out or he gave up the habit of smoking (dejó de fumar.)

The same for go on to do something (else) or go on doing something (continue with the same action).

> He went on to studying a new topic. (he took up new studies) (Pasó a estudiar un tema nuevo.)

> He went on studying for years. (continued) (Siguió estudiando durante años.)

35. MODAL VERBS

ABILITY — CAN / COULD / BE ABLE

PERMISSION — CAN / MAY / COULD / BE ALLOWED TO

POSSIBILITY — MAY / MIGHT / COULD

CERTAINTY — MUST / BOUND TO BE / SURE TO BE / CERTAIN TO BE / CAN'T BE

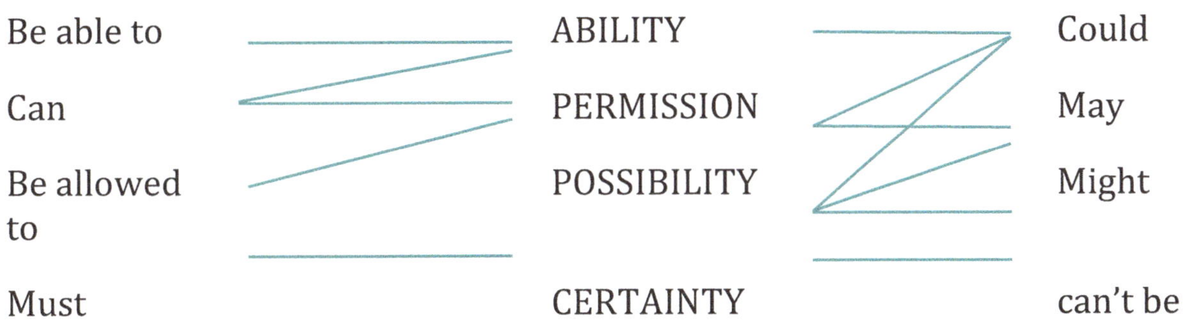

Be able to	ABILITY	Could
Can	PERMISSION	May
Be allowed to	POSSIBILITY	Might
Must	CERTAINTY	can't be

Many learners get very confused with the topic of modals in English, principally because there are so many of them. One way to go through them is to take each modal separately and explore how they are formed and their uses. For example, firstly I would talk through CAN and COULD and the alternative to these BE ABLE TO. Then I would take MAY, MIGHT and explore those. Then MUST and HAVE TO and in this way go step by step building them up. The second way to look at modals and with a more advanced learner, who already has knowledge of them, would be to help learners brainstorm the multiple uses that modals may have. The coaching conversation would entail setting up the classifications, for example ABILITY, PERMISSION, POSSIBILITY and then getting the learner involved in discovering which modals could fall into each classification. In the lower part of this visual, the words could be placed in those positions and then ask the learner to draw the corresponding lines to really consolidate their understanding of all the uses.

36. OBLIGATIONS - MODAL VERBS OF OBLIGATION

POSITIVE	Strongest ↑	NEGATIVE
MUST		
HAVE TO		MUSTN'T
HAVE GOT TO		
		SHOULDN'T
SHOULD		OUGHTN'T TO
OUGHT TO		HAD BETTER NOT
HAD BETTER		BE NOT SUPPOSED TO
BE SUPPOSED TO		
		DON'T HAVE TO
NEED		DON'T NEED TO/NEEDN'T
IT IS NECESSARY		DIDN'T NEED TO (and didn't do it)
	↓	NEEDN'T HAVE (but did actually do it!)
POSITIVE	Weakest	NEGATIVE

This visual is a great way for learners to classify the strength of the obligation and the modal to use for each scenario. The interesting and key point is that the order of strength differs in a negative statement (HAVE TO goes down in strength in the negative). This is an essential table to do with German speakers as there is great confusion with MUSSEN in positive statements and negative statements.

37. PHRASAL VERB FAMILIES (examples of how to create groups)

This could be a good way of getting learners to play with the creation of phrasal verbs and exploring the possible prepositions that could come together with the verbs to then create the phrasal verb. It could also be used for learners to create a visual that brings them the most used combinations. The tables created could be exactly how the learner wants and needs them to be, with colour coding or underlining, whatever works better for the coachee. The coach would need to really ask powerful questions to stimulate the coachee´s imagination on how to create this to make it more effective for him/her.

Get across | Get round | Get at | Get away | Get away with | Get back | Get by | Get down | Get off | Get on | Get on with | Get out of | Get over | Get round to | Get through	Break down | Break into | Break off | Break out | Break through | Break up	Wear off | Wear out
Set down | Set in | Set off|out | Set off | Set out | Set up	Let down | Let in | Let off | Let off | Let out	Cut across | Cut down | Cut down on | Cut in | Cut off | Cut up
Bring about | Bring in | Bring on | Bring off | Bring out | Bring round | Bring up	Look after | Look for | Look in | Look into | Look out | Look through | Look up | Look up to	Come across | Come across | Come off | Come about | Come out | Come round | Come around | Come to | Come up against
	Give away | Give away | Give back | Give in | Give in to | Give out | Give up | Give up	Go away | Go around | Go back | Go back on | Go down with | Go for | Go in for | Go into | Go off (2) | Go on (2) | Go on with | Go out | Go over|through | Go through with | Go with | Go without

38. PHRASAL VERB PREPOSITIONS

Exploring the subtle meanings of the preposition

IN	(gives feeling of)	OUT	(gives feeling of)
Bring in	introduce	Eat out	outside/opposite of
inside			
Participate in	involve	Shut out	exclude
Go in	enter/into/inside	Wear out	exhaust/run out of
		Bring out	introduce something
		Clean out	complete/finish

UP	(gives feeling of)	DOWN	(gives feeling of)
Go up	upward movement	Sit down	downward movement
Shoot up	rise/increase/improve decrease/drop/deteriorate	Go down	
Use up	deplete /finish	Close down	end/complete/stop
Draw up	come near/approach	Talk down at	negative/condescending

ON	(gives feeling of)	OFF	(gives feeling of)
Put on	attach/dress	Move off	move away/separate
Turn on	in function/opposite of OFF	Come off	detach/lose contact
Go on	continue	Go off	rot/go bad
Decide on	concrete/more weight/assume	Set off	detonate/trigger/start
Get on	board/alight	Call off	stop/cancel
		Bring off	reach success/achieve

One of the greatest difficulties with phrasal verbs is the way that we introduce them to learners. Here I am proposing to create a very subtle way of taking one preposition at a time and have a conversation with the learner about the possible meanings that this preposition would bring to a verb. If you can get the learner to intuitively sense the meaning that the prepositional gives, then it will help the learner to contextualise new phrasal verbs faster.

SAMPLE COACHING CONVERSATION

P - Today we have said that we would come into the topic of phrasal verbs. How do you feel about that?

P - I would like to propose that we will do this from a different standpoint today and we will take one preposition at a time. The reason for this is because the preposition itself changes the meaning of the verb and there may be slightly different perspectives or trends in that change of meaning.

PQ - So, if we think of the most common prepositions IN, ON, OFF, OUT, UP, DOWN, which one would you like us to focus on first?

P and C - OK, then, we will start with ON. I would say we could focus on five different perspectives or "feeling" that this preposition can give. Can I ask you if you have any examples of phrasal verbs with ON?

A - Great yes, to carry on. If we think about this one a moment, what meaning is ON bringing to the verb?

CL - Yes, absolutely right, it brings the feeling of continuation or that we continue to do something. So, in fact we could say that the first feeling that ON bring is "to continue doing".

PQ - How would you like us to note this down? OK so a table with ON at the top and then four rows underneath.

ON perspective	Example PVs
1. continue	Carry on, go on, keep on, soldier on...

A - What other phrasal verbs can you think off that would also reflect that meaning on "continuation"... excellent, go on, keep on – may I share an unusual one with you? To soldier on, means to keep on with the battle... what do you think about those?

A - Great, now let us move to some more examples of verbs with ON to discover another meaning that ON brings. Any come to mind?

PQ - Super, yes, to put on meaning to get dressed. So, what do you think is the perspective here? Yes, you could say that – it could be to get dressed or to even to add or attach something. What other verbs would have that sort of feeling with ON?

So, we can add these to the table, super!

ON perspective	Example PVs
1. continue	Carry on, go on, keep on, soldier on…
2. attach/connect/dress	Put on, add on, build on, try on, hold on, lean on

A - Now any other aspects or perspective that you can think of?

T - May I share with you, that ON could also bring the feeling of "functioning" – for example to turn on the radio. What do you think about that? Any others that you can think of?

A - Yes, we could also say to put on the radio in that sense too! What else? Yes we could even say to BE ON or to switch on. If I could add one more, I could also say to come on. So, lets add these to the list.

ON - perspective	Example PVs
1. continue	Carry on, go on, keep on, soldier on…
2. attach/dress	Put on, add on, build on, try on
3. functioning/opposite of OFF	Turn on, put on, switch on, be on

P and T - Next, and this one may be more difficult to sense, but if I can explain it, I would say it is the feeling of something becoming more concrete or something being added, when we use it with some verbs. May I give you the example of decide on doing something. Here I could also say I have decided to go to France, but by adding ON it feels more concrete, I have decided on going to France, almost like there is more weight to it and more determination. May I give you another example, I have taken on more work. This gives me the feeling of more weight, more concrete.

T - I could also add here – this is weighing on me, which means that it is something that causes me stress and is a burden to me. I could even use it in the sense of something catching on – so if I say my idea is catching on, it means it is becoming more crystalised and accepted and people are assuming it and it becomes more concrete.

ON perspective	Example PVs
1. continue	Carry on, go on, keep on, soldier on…
2. attach/dress	Put on, add on, build on, try on
3. functioning/opposite of OFF	Turn on, put on, switch on, be on
4. concrete/more weight/depend	Decide on, catch on, weigh on, take on

A - Finally, we have an easy category and I think you probably know this one. What about when we get on a bus?

C and T - Yes absolutely we can use it to give the feeling on "boarding" – can you think of other phrasal verbs like that one? Yes, jump on, climb on. May I say this could also be used metaphorically – The teacher jumped on the student who was talking at the back. This does not the teacher physically jumped on the student but, definitely, we can use it in the metaphorical sense. What do you think about that?

ON - perspective	Example PVs
1. continue	Carry on, go on, keep on, soldier on…
2. attach/dress	Put on, add on, build on, try on
3. functioning/opposite of OFF	Turn on, put on, switch on, be on
4. concrete/more weight/depend	Decide on, catch on, weigh on, take on
5. boarding	Get on, climb on, jump on

PQ - Now how about we really explore what all of these verbs mean in your language and also explore if any prepositions are used with those verbs, just out of curiosity to see if there is any correspondence or similarities?

PQ - How are you feeling with all of these? How about we look at some other phrasal verbs with ON in some sentences and you try and work out the meaning that they have?

FINAL NOTE FROM RACHEL

As language educators one of our greatest missions is to discover how to help people to learn languages in the most effective and efficient way for that learner or group of learners.

In my own experience, by using professional coaching as the communicative vehicle and by adapting everything we do, so that it follows the neuroscientific research plus all that we now know from the science of learning, neuropsychology plus emotional intelligence, we can truly create and cocreate learning to be a totally different experience than ever before.

Bringing back the joy to language learning is one of my major missions in life and no doubt, it is also your mission too.

I do hope you have enjoyed exploring this brain-friendly resources book and that you are now one step closer to delivering any grammatical area or any part of the language through brain-friendly Neurolanguage Coaching conversations using the PACT PQC educational coaching model.

Wishing you and your learners every success in your cocreations!

Education is not the filling of a pail, but the lighting of a fire.

William Butler Yeats

www.ingramcontent.com/pod-product-compliance
Lightning Source LLC
Chambersburg PA
CBHW061100170426
43201CB00025B/2424